Tears for the
Smaller Dragon

Tears for the Smaller Dragon

The Story of Jim and Jean Livingston

Jean Livingston

Christian Publications, Inc.
Camp Hill, Pennsylvania

Christian Publications
3825 Hartzdale Drive, Camp Hill, PA 17011

Faithful, biblical publishing since 1883

ISBN: 0-87509-703-0

97 98 99 00 01   5 4 3 2 1

Cover portrait by Karl Foster

This is
dedicated to the
Second Wave, a team of young missionaries sent to Vietnam
by The Christian and Missionary Alliance between 1956 and 1968.
To our co-workers, each of whom could write their own tale of courage and
adventure, to our brothers and sisters as we labored together for the
the kingdom of God in the Land of the Smaller Dragon, we salute you:
Dale Herendeen, Leroy and Nancy Josephson, Dave & Jeanne Frazier,
George and Elsie Wood, Betty and Garth Hunt, Betty
and Ken White, Stan and Joanne Lemon,
Svea and Bob Henry, Barbara and Spencer Sutherland,
Marnie and Bill Mock, Bob and Elsie Davis
Ruth and Gale Erickson, Tom and Donna
Stebbins, Marge and Ted Cline,
Charlotte and Woody
Stemple, John and
Penny Hall, Irene
and Gail Fleming,
Tina and Wes
Schelander,
Ginny and
Orrel Steinkamp,
Joyce and
Bob McNeel,
E.G. and
Charlie Long,
Joan Downs,
Lillian and
Dick Phillips,
Ellen and Ross
Duncan, Sharon
Allwine, Keith
Kayser, Joan
and Norm Johnson,
Donna and Reg Reimer,
June and Harold Collins,
Beth and Rick Drummond,
Dick and Marge Pendell,
Elsie and Merle Douglas, Dixie
and Victor Oliver, Helen and Dave
Douglas, Dawn Deets, David Beack,
Bernice and Ken Swain, Carol Steckel,
Bob and Bobbie Reed, Jackie and C.G. Ingram,
Gloria and Fred Kleinhen.
And to our four children who loved Vietnam
and her people:
Stephen Michael,
Nancy Ellen,
Ramona Joy,
and Tara
Suzan-
ne.

Contents

Acknowledgments

I am deeply grateful for my husband Jim who gave hundreds of hours working side by side with me in the writing of this story. He was a great source of encouragement during those final months in the refugee camp when the situation was anything but ideal for writing—no electricity, no water, inconveniences, interruptions, security threats and multiple distractions.

Jim kept the focus of our writing and reminded me constantly of the greater picture—joy in service of our Lord Jesus Christ.

Special mention goes to Mrs. Pattie Peters and Rev. James Snyder who gave valuable advice in the drafting stage of this story. Amateurs we are and grateful we are for their timely help.

Introduction

The former South Vietnamese soldier stood in silence, gazing over the placid waters. *The sea is beautiful today,* thought Giang (YANG). Proud to be born a North Vietnamese, he included Ha Long village as part of his inheritance. *This is my birthplace, my home, the place where the dragon came down,* he mused.

The young man shivered and adjusted the dangling sleeve which hung loosely by his side. Out in the Gulf of Tonkin, tall, rocky spines rose from the dark waters. Each rock was a separate sentinel, indeed very much like the spine of a dragon. Vietnamese mythology credits these rocks to an ancient dragon—what we see as merely unusual erosion.

The war was over and Vietnam was united now, but it had taken twenty-one long years, and at such a terrible price. For Giang, the cost included the loss of his father, his younger brother and the family property as they fled south during the communist takeover. Worst of all, he had lost his right arm.

Oh, Vietnam, Vietnam! Sadness seems to be our

constant companion. Will it always be this way?
Giang turned and slowly walked away.

Giang's homeland had once been a con-
quered vassal of that Greater Dragon to the
north, China, which ruled the Viet people for
1,000 years. But one day, the Smaller Dragon
dared to spit fire in the face of the larger one
and forced him back across his borders.

Glancing at a map, one can see that the Vietnamese coastline does indeed resemble the
shape of a dragon. The Vietnamese see themselves as small. Yes! But they also see themselves as a people characterized with a
dragon's authority and power.

In 1911, missionaries first arrived in the Land
of the Smaller Dragon with the message of joy
which made possible the transformation of lives.
Many years later, when the Evangelical Church
of Vietnam (an independent, indigenous national church founded by and closely associated
with The Christian and Missionary Alliance) was
already strong and growing, Jim and I arrived as
part of a new wave of young missionaries. Our
husband-wife team has been gently led by our
wonderful Lord in working with the Vietnamese
people in Vietnam, in the refugee camps of the
Philippines and in the United States. We have
been privileged to live and work in Southeast
Asia's amazing, contemporary history, side by
side and in the midst of the fighting, the blood-

shed and the rehabilitation.

The Little Dragon of this book is symbolic of both the land and her people. Those pointed peaks rising like the spine of an ancient dragon out of the ocean at Ha Long are characteristic of Vietnamese believers. Though often with tear-filled eyes, their witness remains joyful and effective. Their authority is the Word of God and their secret weapons are threefold: prevailing prayer, bold tenacity in the face of incredible odds and fantastic joy. No wonder they rise undaunted above the waters of affliction.

One Spirit-filled pastor, recalling his six years of incarceration in a communist prison and the suffering of the Church, laughed and said, "They try, but they can't stop us!"

Ours too is a story sprinkled with tears—not tears of remorse and woe, but tears which became droplets of joy. For us, ministry with the Vietnamese people has been a time of "going out weeping," and it continues to this very hour to be a time of "returning with songs of joy."

> *"Those who sow in tears will reap*
> *with songs of joy. He who goes out*
> *weeping, carrying seed to sow, will return*
> *with songs of joy, carrying sheaves*
> *with him."* (Psalm 126:5-6)

1

Three Sons,
Three Mothers,
Three Conflicts

It was hot and sticky in Saigon. The year—
1966. Jim was serving as a civilian chaplain in
Vietnam's largest military hospital, the 4,000-
bed Cong Hoa (Cam WA) Hospital, located at
the extreme end of the jet runway of Tan San
Nhut (Tung Shung NYUK) Airport. Due to the
escalation of military operations ranging as far as
200 miles in any direction from Saigon, the hospital wards overflowed with the wounded, sometimes two patients to a bed.

Walking down the veranda of Ward E that
now accommodated more than 200 men with
serious leg wounds, Jim stopped suddenly and
held his breath. Piercing cries were coming
from someone near the window. Compelled by

those repeated shrieks of agony, Jim entered the long, dismal room lined with twenty or more hospital beds.

A male nurse was bending over the writhing body of a young Army of the Republic of Vietnam (ARVN) soldier. A small utility cart held scissors, cotton, alcohol and several rolls of sterile bandages. This was the first bandage change on the boy's amputated leg since surgery and the nurse was removing the dry, bloodstained bandages that stuck tightly to his raw stump.

Instinctively Jim moved to the bedside. Looking down into a face twisted with pain, he gently began consoling the soldier who seemed to be hardly more than a kid of seventeen.

"There, my brother, lie still. Don't be afraid. In a few moments the pain will be less."

Then, on impulse, even as the nurse continued working, Jim grasped the boy's amputated half leg just above the bloody stump. *Maybe by gripping the leg tightly somehow the horrible pain might be lessened,* he thought.

The stub looked like a hunk of raw meat. The nurse continued his unpleasant chore of pouring pink antiseptic liquid onto the open wound. This caused more writhing. Finally, clean muslins replaced the soiled ones.

Share Jesus, some word of comfort, Jim thought to himself. *But is this the time? This kid is so full of pain he can't even lie still. I'll let him rest now and come back in a few days.*

Several days later, Anh Trong (An TRUM), the boy soldier with the amputated leg, was quiet as Jim approached his bed. *What a gentle lad this is!* he thought.

The young soldier was ready to talk now. His mother was Cambodian, his father Vietnamese. They lived in the southern delta near the Cambodian border. His only complaint was, "I have lost my leg. What am I going to do? I want to go back to my buddies and fight!" He knew and Jim knew that this would never happen.

Now a week later, it was the right time to share Christ with Anh Trong. His heart was tender and ready, and with genuine compassion Jim told the young soldier about the wounds of Jesus Christ, the Son of Duc Chua Troi (Dook CHOOA Troi), the Great God of the Heavens. This Jesus had also suffered, not to defend His country from communism, but to redeem sinful man. Anh Trong gladly accepted Christ as his Savior. That day a hospital bed of tears became a place of faith and peace. And in heaven the angels sang songs of joy!

But deep in South Vietnam's delta country, a thin, little woman was waiting with mounting fear and apprehension. Trong's mother had received the brief letter informing the family of his severe wounds. The conflict on the road to Tay Ninh (Tay NIN) had claimed one of her son's legs.

"My boy left home a mere lad," the mother mused sadly, "but he will return as if old and maimed, crippled for life."

Our family was in Vietnam as missionaries with The Christian and Missionary Alliance. We were caught in the war. Conflict would be ever present. But, for us, another conflict was equally real, even paramount. We were in the Land of the Smaller Dragon to recapture precious souls long held by the despot Satan. And a part of that spiritual struggle would be a willingness to be separated from our children for several months each year.

It was the second Sunday in December 1962 and just one more day until our six-year-old son Steve would return home from his first semester at Dalat School. Dalat was the boarding school for our missionary kids (MKs) located in the city by that name in the cool highlands of Vietnam. MKs came to Dalat from Cambodia, Thailand, Laos and, of course, Vietnam.

Eighteen weeks before, we had said our goodbyes to this little boy who was the apple of his father's eye. Steve was happy at Dalat, enjoying his new friends from Thailand, Larry Persons and Daryl Dreger. And there were all his old buddies including Peter Dutton and David Collins. Jim and I had awaited Steve's scanty "dictated-to-dorm-parents" letters each week with much anticipation.

Now, on that warm December day, little three-year-old sister Kim Hoa and I had gone to the morning worship service at the Quang Ngai (Kwang NGEYE) Vietnamese church as usual. We sat on the front row of the ladies side of the church near the rear door. The men and boys sat on the opposite side of the building. This segregated seating arrangement was the Vietnamese custom during that era.

Pastor Linh (LIN) had just finished his sermon when suddenly our friend, Sergeant Dillard Eads, appeared at the door near where Kim Hoa and I were seated.

What is Sergeant Eads doing here? I wondered silently. I stared at him with surprise since our U.S. soldier friends never had cause to attend the Tin Lanh (Teen LAN) Good News Vietnamese Church. They could not understand the Vietnamese language.

During the early days of the U.S. troop buildup in Central Vietnam, the troops had no chaplain, Protestant or Catholic, assigned to our province. Often on Sunday evenings we had entertained small groups of American soldiers at our home. They enjoyed the singing, Bible study and light refreshments. But most of all they seemed to enjoy our children.

Sergeant Eads was motioning for me to come outside. Little Kim Hoa preceded me, for she regarded all the guys in uniform at the Military Advisory Assistance Group (MAAG) compound as her special buddies.

"Where's Jim?" he asked without greeting.

"He's not here. He went to Saigon to pick up Steve."

"Oh," continued the sergeant. "Uh . . . well, a chopper crashed against a mountain out west of Chau O (Chao O) last night. Got caught in a downdraft or somethin'. Anyway, there were eight on board—all presumed dead. The first body has been recovered and his dog tag shows he's Protestant. They brought him to the airstrip already and the colonel sent me to get Jim. So . . . he ain't here. You better come. Colonel said that boy's just gotta have some kind of a memorial service or somethin'."

"Stunned" would have been an understated adjective describing my reaction, to say the least.

"I . . . me . . . ? I don't know if I can," I stammered.

"Look, Jean, the colonel said for me to come and get someone. So let's go! On the double!"

"Sergeant, I will ask our Vietnamese pastor to come along if you think it's all right."

"OK, but make it snappy!"

A short five-minute ride by jeep and we were at the airstrip. Several twin-rotored, troop-carrying Chinook choppers were perched on the runway like huge brown locusts waiting for some signal to take to the sky. Our jeep came to an abrupt stop and we hopped out.

Serious-faced men in battle fatigues were

milling around. The colonel came toward me, but it was Sergeant Eads who spoke.

"Sir! This is the missionary's wife, Jean Livingston. Chaplain Jim's in Saigon today, sir."

We shook hands without a word and walked together to the drab, olive-colored military ambulance with the large red cross painted on the top and sides. The colonel motioned for the rest of the troops to join us at the rear of the ambulance. One of the men threw back the heavy canvas flap which hung over the open space. Stretchers were stacked one on top of another in rack-like order. On the top rack two jungle combat boots jutted out from under a bloodstained army blanket.

"Go ahead!" commanded the colonel, looking squarely at me.

There had been no prior training for this hour, no one to run to for advice, no one to phone and request prayer—and no husband nearby to perform this grim task which was obviously a military chaplain's job, not mine.

"The LORD is my shepherd; I shall not want .. . . He leadeth me. . . . Yea, though I walk through the valley of the shadow of death, I will fear no evil: for thou art with me. . . ."

There were a few moments of silence, each participant wrapped in his own private thoughts and fears. Then I said, "Pastor Linh, will you please pray? Pray in Vietnamese. It's all right."

The whining sound of the fretful and restless

wind was the only hymn sung during this brief, but solemn ceremony.

It wasn't until later that same evening, safe in our mission home and after little Kim Hoa was asleep under her mosquito net, that I allowed myself time to ponder a bit. I wondered about that soldier boy on that stretcher. *Did I hear correctly? Was the name Hamilton?* The image of those sprawled army boots are indelibly imprinted on my mind. *Why me, Lord? Why was I called to stand at the feet of that dead soldier today? What a sad privilege! But why me?*

Then my thoughts switched course and I wished I could cry out over the vast ocean that separated us in Vietnam from the homeland in the United States. I wanted to call to a mother who may not have yet received the tragic news from the United States Department of Defense. With sincere compassion and respect, I wanted to say, "Dear soldier boy's mother, perhaps it would be a comfort to you if you knew that another mother was at your son's side today. Naturally, you could not be at that simple memorial service, but I was there. It wasn't much, but I did what I could. I wept."

At noon the next day the loud clackety-thud of a Huey chopper overhead caused me to look up from my work. Down, down it came as dust and bits of grass and leaves flew in all directions. This was not the first time a chopper had landed in our back yard. A few seconds later I knew why the unexpected visit today.

The first person to be helped down from the back seat was our little son Steve. How many boys can boast that they caught a ride home from school in an army chopper? Smiling from ear to ear, husband Jim had brought me the one thing I needed most to comfort this aching mother's heart. The spirit of heaviness lifted. No more tears. In their place, only sweet joy. My son was home again.

Three mothers whose lives in just a few short hours had been thrown into conflict, conflict so real as to be life-changing. One mother would soon welcome home her brave soldier-son, a lad who had once marched off to war with flags of hope for peace flying deep in his heart. That son would soon return home, but minus one of his legs.

One mother would soon be stricken with devastating grief. She would receive her precious son as well, but he would be in an aluminum casket.

The third mother, who with her husband made that tough decision to send their only son off to a boarding school, now, many years later, rejoices, because time has proven it was the right decision. That son became a missionary-teacher on the campus of Dalat School and was used by God in shaping the lives of other mothers' sons and daughters, the MK's in Southeast Asia.

2

Anything, Anywhere

"Jean, do you go to church?"

It was the spring of 1947, and in fourth period gym class at St. Petersburg High School we were still practicing basketball. Passing and shooting had made me hot and sweaty. While standing on the sidelines trying to catch my breath, a friendly, dark-haired girl surprised me with that question.

"Oh . . . well . . . er . . . I go to the big First Methodist Church downtown!" I bluffed, knowing full well that our family rarely attended church except at Easter or Christmastime. Once a year my dad would have his white suit cleaned and, looking stiff and most uncomfortable, would go to church on Mother's Day in memory of his mother who had died at the time of his birth. Our family just wasn't much interested in church. There was no way that I could know, standing there in sweaty gym clothes, talking to a girl I hardly knew, that the conversation she began would change the course of my entire life.

"Really? Me too! I go to Northside Methodist Church," said Mary Lou.

Actually, I do not know how it all came about, but within the next few minutes somehow I had committed myself to going to prayer meeting with Mary Lou. And so, when 7 o'clock came, I found myself in the back seat of an old Ford V-8 with Mary Lou, a guy named Bill, plus another "steady" couple. I felt like the oddball indeed, not knowing if this was some kind of a sandwich date or what!

But a few minutes later my feelings of awkwardness were forgotten. Mere words can never express my first impressions of this small group of people who called themselves not just Methodists, but born-again Christians. Almost at once I felt the awesome magnet of their love. I simply had no idea that this kind of warmth existed in churches.

Old Brother Masters warmly greeted us teens with a sincerity that was surprisingly new to me. Little Aunt Iva, the piano player with only three fingers on her left hand, could bang out tunes on that old upright till it shook with joy. She was indeed everybody's aunt and proceeded to put her arms around Mary Lou and Bill for her biweekly hug.

The Gowdys were there too. They were the youth sponsors who in the future would have a profound effect on my life. Mr. Gowdy, though painfully stooped from rheumatoid arthritis, had a quiet sense of humor and joked and laughed easily. You could always see a Christlike gentleness in his face. When the singing started, I could hear his low, velvet voice from where he sat in his special chair by the window.

Prayer time was another surprise, for it was not just the preacher who led in prayer, but everyone was invited to pray "as the Spirit leads." Mrs. Gowdy just talked to the Lord like He was standing right there with us in that little one-room church.

From the back of the room, old Brother Shutt, nearly blind and wearing thick spectacles, managed to get down on his knees between the benches to pray. There seemed to be tears in his voice, but it was beautiful. The old man prayed that we would all "drink deep out of the wells of salvation."

Friendly? Yes, those dear folks simply demolished all my barriers and fears of being in new and strange church meetings. Joyful? Yes, they had found something, but it was not like the excited emotion that one sees at a ballgame. Love? Here in that little church, where everyone seemed important to everyone else, where no one was overlooked and where the worth of every person contributed to the good of the whole, yes, their love was indeed unique. Clearly I had just stepped onto the threshold of an amazing yet sublime discovery. I saw for the first time that in the good company of Jesus' saints there was a divine, delightful, heaven-given joy. Mary Lou, the Gowdys, old Brother Shutt, little Aunt Iva—all those folks at Northside Methodist Church had something that I had never seen or experienced before.

During the months that followed, my heart became fixed. I accepted with utmost simplicity the basic Christian doctrines which taught that man is a sinner and in need of a Savior. Especially did I find much help from the sharing time after church on Sunday evenings. At that time, the youth room would be darkened except for the light from a small candle's reflection on a handsome picture of Jesus on the table.

During "sharing hour," the young people sang choruses and shared how the Lord had used them during the past week to witness to friends and family. I listened. I was learning that a Christian walked and talked with Jesus, not just on Sunday but all week long, and in this special relationship there was much joy.

I graduated from high school in the spring of 1948, still not quite seventeen, and applied for admission at Mound Park Nurses' Training School. I was very politely rejected. "Too young," they said.

Naturally, I was embarrassed to face my friends who were headed for college or for employment in jobs with a promising future. It was difficult to see the hand of the Lord upon my life at that time.

There was yet one other perplexing problem that gnawed away in the secret place of my heart, something about which I could not find the courage to speak to anyone. And I whispered this ever so softly, "Am I truly a Christian yet?"

For sure, I saw myself as being very different from the girl I had been a year before. The direction of my life had been changed. My friends were different; the way I used my free time was different. Nothing was the same anymore. I was reading my Bible twice, sometimes three times a day, so hungry was I for more of this Jesus of Galilee.

I remember the first time I learned about tithing. I thought, *Well, if this is God's plan for His Church, then I shall begin tithing my paycheck this week.* And I did. Furthermore, each summer for the next four years I gladly gave a secret love-gift to the Lord—one entire week's salary—so much was my desire to serve Him any way I could.

But in all those months of attending Northside I never had a personal "altar experience," and this bothered me. Still, there was a genuine burden that others, my family in particular, would come to know Christ.

One day, with fear and trepidation, I found the courage to go to Spring Market to try and persuade my daddy to follow Christ. I went with great expectations. God would prepare my dad's heart and give me the right spiritual gems to say when I got there.

The grocery store was empty when I arrived and Daddy was whistling away behind the meat counter.

"Well, hello there. What brings you here?"

"I just got off work, Daddy. I rode my bike. I . . . er . . . er . . ." But no golden nuggets fell from my mouth. Where was the special anointing that was supposed to come? We had sung the song, "I may not pray like Peter; I may not preach like Paul, but I can tell the love of Jesus, how He died to save us all." But it was not happening! I was speechless with fear and absolutely ignorant as to how to share my faith.

Finally, after what seemed like an eternity, I started to cry and I blurted out words that were inappropriate and crude, "Daddy, I want you to stop smoking and go to church!"

I stood there for a brief, confused moment, absolutely mortified at what I had just done and fearing that I had most likely ruined the possibility of my daddy ever finding Christ as his Savior. I did not wait to see his reaction, but turned and ran out of the store.

I could hardly face my parents that night at the supper table; I was so ashamed. It would be almost two years before what was sown that afternoon as tears would come forth as pearls.

And then He called me.

It happened during the year I spent waiting

to grow up and enter nurses' training. The only missionary I had ever heard about was actor Spencer Tracy and his classic line, "Dr. Livingstone, I presume!"

On January 30, 1949, the fifth Sunday of the month and the one we called World Service Sunday, Lucy Lyons gave a speech in Sunday school. It was a report taken from a magazine about foreign missions.

At home that evening I took time as usual to read God's Word before going to my bedroom. There by my bedside, I knelt to pray.

A few sentences of praise, a request about work tomorrow, and then quite suddenly an assault of uninvited thoughts began.

A missionary? Lord, is this You speaking? No, my mind seems to be reeling! Me? Be a missionary? No, Lord! This is just an emotional trip, the influence of Lucy's talk. Besides, I don't think I like missionaries. They wear unstylish clothes and pin their hair in a bun on the back of their heads. I could never be a missionary.

Quite involuntarily, I began to weep. There was no explanation for those tears. Soon my weeping turned to sobbing. I cried uncontrollably. Never had I felt so melted in the presence of the Lord.

A missionary? But Lord, have I not told You that I shall be happy to be Your nurse? Only a couple more months, Lord. I'll be eighteen and then I'll reapply for admission at Mound Park Hospital. This time they will accept me. Lord . . . Lord . . . ?

I do not know how long I knelt there. I had ceased to pray. I just wept. The night had become ever so quiet. The Florida crickets had ceased their tunes, but my silent tears were unending and brought with them an experience not unlike that of surgery.

Oh, my Lord, what am I to do? The long-standing desire of my life to be a nurse was being gently and tenderly removed from my heart, yet I felt no anger toward God, only the deepest love possible. And as He continued the melting process, He called me to missions.

Yes! Yes, Lord Jesus, I will be Your missionary. But this will be impossible unless You empower me with Your Spirit. Fill me now, and I promise—anything, Lord Jesus, anything. Anywhere, Lord Jesus, anywhere. I am Yours completely.

Immediately there flowed into my soul peace, the Peace who is a Person. I rose from my knees quite literally out of breath as if I had been racing in some heavenly marathon. My transaction with my heavenly Father was finished. We had made a contract.

Looking back on that unforgettable night, I wonder if my heavenly Father was smiling. If it would have been possible to read the fine print of that agreement, I would have seen that in only two years I would meet another missionary-in-the-making. The two of us would serve the Lord together in a land which up to that point in time very few Americans had ever heard of: Vietnam, the Land of the Smaller Dragon.

3

Just One Little Kid

I met Jim Livingston in the fall of 1951 during our third year at Asbury College. He asked me to attend a Saturday evening concert. Jim was quite shy and let me do most of the talking, but over the next few weeks I would learn much more about this boy from Alabama.

James H. Livingston was the oldest of four children born to Bess Lou Ethridge and James Robert Livingston. On his birthday, February 21, 1931, Robert suggested that the baby be named after himself, but young mother Bess wanted a more noble-sounding name and reached back into her family's Civil War past to pick it out.

"Robert," she said, "I want to name the baby Haley. My great Uncle Haley was a fine man, a soldier decorated for heroism in the Confederate Army during the Civil War. Got a medal

22

and a big sword!" Bess laughed softly. "Let's name our son James Haley Livingston."

The war years of 1941-45 were filled with a kind of serious fascination for a boy growing up in the deep south. Two miles from Jimmy Livingston's home in the suburbs of Birmingham, Alabama, skilled hands guided the assembly line, and every hour and thirty minutes a B-24 four-engine bomber, fresh off the assembly line, droned to the sky destined for Newfoundland, then Britain and the bombing runs over Hitler's Germany.

Meatless Tuesdays were encouraged, and school kids were sent throughout the neighborhood to sell eighteen-dollar war bonds. Drives to collect scrap metal and newspapers were common in those years too. Jimmy and his friends joined the efforts with enthusiasm. They prided themselves in knowing the designs of warships and dive bombers.

Near the close of the twentieth century, historians would look back and write that these war years were America's finest hour in a century otherwise best characterized as dismal, dark, full of war and utterly tragic. But Jimmy was troubled about the course of the war. He wondered if Pastor Connor's Marine son would return from fighting in the the South Pacific.

How much does a child understand about war and death, about refugees and hurting people? Most youngsters cannot put their feelings into words, but over the years God has His ways of building into them an allowance for difficult times, a kind of a preparation for tears. Some day Jimmy would experience the trauma of another war and come to know firsthand places like Chu Lai (Choo LIE), Binh Son (Bin SHUNG), Quang Ngai (Kwang NGEYE), Son Nam (Shung NAM) and Corregidor, and even that place on the radio evening news called Bataan which would one day become his home.

For poor families like the Livingstons, ready cash was always scarce and work opportunities had to be snatched wherever possible. At age nine, already growing tall and strong, Jimmy brought in coal and firewood for six elderly ladies, and his weekly tithe came to five cents.

His interest in missions caught on early, and on the brown missions faith pledge envelopes he scrawled, "Robert and Betty Adams, French West Africa, 5 cents."

Jimmy remembers one summer when a cloud of heavy sadness hung low over the Livingston house. Four-year-old Robert had been his daddy's special delight, but the little boy took sick very suddenly. Mother Bess took him to the big Baptist Hospital. The doctors seemed baffled, and for more than twenty days they could not seem to diagnose the cause of little Robert's severe fevers. A few days later, Robert went to be with Jesus. Everyone cried, but Jimmy's daddy grieved without consolation and would never be the same.

Unable to cope with personal tragedy, Robert began to drink after the unexpected loss of his son. He would work for three or four weeks, and then depression would hit him. Those were lost weekends in the Livingston home.

The star of the Saturday night "Hit Parade" was singing "Into Each Life Some Rain Must Fall." Bess Livingston could have easily sung the second line, "but too much has fallen in mine!" But she didn't. She was a woman of quiet nobility. I remember Jim once saying to a group of more than a thousand Vietnamese soldiers, "If I had never seen or held a Bible in my hand, I would have known and loved God because of what I saw in my mother's life."

Bess's walk with the Lord began one hot summer evening when she was invited to go to a revival meeting being held by the flamboyant radio preacher, Dr. Glenn V. Tingley. The Word found fertile soil in the heart of this young mother. Bess had already lost one child and was now losing a husband to liquor. She was grasping for help and desperately needed a Savior and a Friend.

Now, as Bess began to grow in Christ, her first desire was to live a quiet, godly life before her husband. Her second desire was to lead her children to know Christ as a living Person. One evening, Bess took her brood to a gospel tent meeting which included singing, trombone playing and a message by Charles Wisser, one

of Dr. Tingley's preacher boys fresh out of
Nyack Missionary Training Institute.

The crowds were small, and by the end of the
week there were no converts—well, only one, a
six-year-old boy.

But wait! The young preacher, Chuck, did
not know the rest of the story. The very next
day after inviting Jesus to come into his heart,
Mother Bess watched with absolute amazement as her son witnessed to his school buddy
and tried to persuade him to receive Christ
too. Does a child really know what he is doing
when he asks the heavenly Father to forgive
him of his sins? Little Jimmy Livingston knew.

Shortly thereafter, the Livingston family
moved across Birmingham to the suburbs near
East Lake where the children spent most of
their growing up years. Barrett Elementary
School was only one block from home.

"Jimmy! Mike! Jane! Are ya ready? Let's go!"
the neighborhood children called from the
sidewalk in front of the Livingston home. But
mother was not ready to send her little scholars
to school yet.

"Come, kneel down. We'll pray before you
go," she called.

Prayer was as much a part of going to school
as was hot oatmeal, toast and Blue Horse note-
book paper. Sometimes Mother Bess even
brought the neighborhood kids inside the sitting room to pray with her own children. And
they prayed for their daddy, remembering

Mother's oft-repeated words, "Someday God will wonderfully save your daddy."

Robert never hindered his family from attending services at the little country church, later renamed East Lake Alliance Church, but neither did he want to go himself. Thus, at a time when their own dad was not prepared to be a spiritual role model in the lives of the Livingston children, the saints of East Lake Alliance Church—ordinary godly men and women—were able to model and influence their spiritual growth and character.

One day the kindly pastor offered Jimmy a job as church janitor, and the little church on Third Avenue North became like a midway station between earth and heaven to Jimmy. Whether it was to keep the church clean, to make sure the coal stove was ready for use on Sundays, to cut grass in the summer or to rake leaves in the fall, Jimmy was committed to excellence.

How does God prepare one whom He has chosen to be His servant? Missionaries are made, not born. The life of his mother and the lives of the saints at East Lake Church—like Mr. Sharp, the Sunday school teacher; Bob Lock, a company vice-president; Mr. Thomas, the milkman; the Moppins; the Selbys; Jessie Helms and Perry Bush; and Pastor Roger Connor—all had a significant impact on this one little kid, this missionary-in-the-making.

In a Sunday morning message, Jim stated, "Of all the adults in my home church, I cannot remember a single person whose life lacked integrity. As far as I knew, they were all men and women of deep, practical, down-to-earth righteousness. The modeling influence in my life was profound!"

And thus the Sovereign One often allows those things to happen to His children so that we gradually become acquainted with pain and tears. Jimmy belonged to Jesus, and his Savior was preparing him even in those early years for a ministry of compassion, tears and unusual fruitfulness in the kingdom of God.

4

Called!

Warm, big-hearted and ever conscious of spiritual issues, Mrs. Oshal Heis looked at the book in her hands and pondered. She had watched fourteen-year-old Jimmy Livingston for some time. This boy was the unchallenged leader of a romping troop of neighborhood teens. But Mrs. Heis could see that he had a tender, compassionate heart. Jimmy took his responsibilities in Sunday school and as church custodian very seriously. *I wonder if Jimmy would benefit from reading this biography,* thought Mrs. Heis.

The next Sunday, a copy of *Jonathan Goforth of China* was placed in Jimmy's hands. Now, on Sunday afternoons, Jonathan Goforth became Jimmy's companion. The inspiring saga of the life and ministry of the Goforth family during the days of the Boxer

Rebellion in China captured the boy's mind and stirred his emotions as no other book had ever done.

Missionary conventions at East Lake Church brought many modern-day heroes of the faith into the circle of Jimmy's acquaintances. Their exciting stories of spreading the gospel in strange lands were fascinating. But it was the courage and faith of that stalwart Canadian Presbyterian missionary, Jonathan Goforth, that the Holy Spirit used to quicken Jimmy's heart.

It seemed to Jimmy that every place Goforth went, God's mighty arm was extended in power—healing, salvation, miracles, revival. *What would it be like to experience a continuous outpouring of spiritual power like Goforth?* he wondered.

Now Jimmy was not even considering the ministry as a life vocation. For quite some time he had dreamed about being a political cartoonist. With some training . . . , well, there was definite potential for a future career as a commercial artist some day.

Perhaps our gracious Lord was again smiling as He watched Jimmy travel through the pages of that awesome biography. There was no way he could have known that twenty years down the road he would meet the daughter of that pioneer missionary to China, Mrs. Ruth Jeffrey, by then a missionary with forty-seven years of service with The Christian and Missionary Alliance in Vietnam.

It took four years of gentle, quiet, persuasive, persistent nudging by the Holy Spirit, and the calling finally took full root in Jim's heart. The seventeen-year-old never again questioned his call to lifelong service.

The Livingston family lived simply and had no funds for sending their three children to college. Thus Jim would have to find work if he were going to make it financially. With the hope that some job at Asbury College could be made available for his promising young parishioner, on September 14, 1949, Rev. Roger Conner wrote the registrar: "He has a real experience of conversion and more recently of the sanctifying work of the Holy Spirit. You will find him a humble, earnest seeker after God's best. He comes from a home where a godly mother knows how to pray her children through."

One half mile west of Wilmore and situated on a beautiful crest of one of central Kentucky's endless rolling hillsides was the Asbury College farm. The farm was God's answer to Jim's need for financial assistance.

Known by their dirty jeans and smelly shoes, the "farm boys" were a cross section of what Jim came to believe was the best in America. Big smiling John Thrasher of Indiana, a solid workhorse of a man; "Moose" from West Virginia; quiet, soft-spoken Don Johns of Oklahoma; and loud, brash Charlie Covington from Maryland—these were real farm boys with calloused hands from long hours of disciplined outdoor work. Jim was a novice, a city boy, but his respect for these boys was unbounded.

Jim's first assignment on the college farm was to feed and care for all the Hereford beef calves which were kept separated from the rest of the herd. But taking a hammer in hand to kill a beef cow before butchering, gutting hogs, dehorning calves, shoveling manure and the dusty, detestable job of baling hay were labors totally foreign to the city boy from Birmingham. The other farm boys never let him forget it!

For Jim, soul growth might well have ended one dark, dreary November day. After three days of fever, he was near a point of complete physical exhaustion. Jim fought the temptation to give up, to quit. He was too proud to ask Mr. Witt, the farm manager, for permission to go to bed which would have no doubt invited harassment from ol' Charlie (*Can't you take it, Jimmy boy?*). Then he remembered the milking barn and the bales of hay stacked thirty feet high up in the loft.

Bundled in several layers of clothing, Jim managed to climb to the top of the loft and there, silent and alone before the Lord, he waited. *If God doesn't come to my rescue and grant divine strength to this sick body and discouraged soul, and if God does not give me a supernatural ability to endure this exhausting lifestyle,* Jim thought to himself, *I will just have to quit. I simply have no energy left to go on.*

With a sacrifice of tears he offered himself to the Lord Jesus just as he was: ill with a fever, discouraged with his inability to cope with the rigors of farm life, carrying a full semester load of studies and suffering from that most debilitating disease called homesickness. The young missionary-in-the-making was in the processs of acquiring that most needed character quality called "stickability."

Thus, the matter was settled. The Holy Spirit met and revived an almost extinguished fire in Jim's heart that cold November day. After the "barn experience," every letter written to Jim's family was not only full of tales about his farm life, but also full of praise for the goodness of God, sprinkled with generous amounts of preaching.

Burdened for his unsaved dad, on April 30, 1950, Jim wrote:

> There are two men that I love and respect. I dare say I love these men more than any men I shall ever know. They are to me tops! One is our Savior Jesus Christ, the Son of God. To prove that I love and appreciate what Jesus did in dying on the cross, I am giving my life to His service.
>
> The other man is you, my own dad. You are in many ways, with many talents, admirable, but you are lacking one thing. Upon that thing is what I base my life! If you, Dad, had Jesus Christ's life within, you would be ideal! Meet Jesus, Daddy!

Jim did not inform his folks of the time of his

arrival for the Christmas holidays. He wanted to surprise them. He got off the Greyhound two blocks from home, carried his suitcase up onto the porch and quietly let himself into the house. His intention was to burst inside and yell, "Surprise! Surprise!", but the sounds of a man's sobbing caused his heart to stand still.

Quietly he tiptoed to the door of the bedroom. There, kneeling beside the bed, weeping openly, confessing his sins and accepting Christ as his personal Saviour was Robert, Jim's alcoholic father.

Great tears came to Jim's eyes. He had never seen his dad pray. *My mother's tears have not been in vain,* Jim thought as he pondered the scene. *Sixteen years of believing prayer were not in vain!* Mother Bess's words, "Some day God is going to save your daddy. Just pray!" were being fulfilled right before his very eyes.

Following those marvelous moments of confession and Robert's conversion, there was never a drop of liquor in Jim's house again.

Back at Asbury College, Jim was attracted to the tall girl who had just stepped forward to lead the class in the singing of a few choruses. I was that girl. After class, he stopped me.

"Jean," he said abruptly, "I would like to ask you to attend the Saturday night program. It's a black quartet." There was no let's-get-acquainted talk like, "Hi, How ya doin'?" Just wham! Later when we talked about our awk-

ward meeting, Jim liked to tell his side of getting to know Jeannie with the light brown
hair:

> At that time, Asbury had an unwrittten rule: If a
> professor were more than ten minutes late, the
> class was automatically dismissed. One day, Pro-
> fessor Serrott was late, very late, and I was about
> to collect my books and leave when a tall girl
> stood up and said, "Surely Miss Serrott should be
> here any minute. Why don't we just sing and
> praise the Lord until she arrives?"
>
> "Land sakes," I moaned, "so much for my escape
> to the library!" After watching her a few minutes,
> my disappointment in not getting some unex-
> pected free time began to subside, and I thought,
> *Hey, a girl like this would certainly be a help in the
> ministry!*

During summer vacation between our junior
and senior years, I asked my Methodist pastor
a question that was heavy on my mind: "What
in the world is The Christian and Missionary
Alliance?" I was greatly relieved when my pastor told me that this denomination believed as
we did with a strong emphasis on overseas missions. That was music to my ears, for by then I
was definitely interested in the tall boy from
Birmingham. Though quite different in person-
ality, we were from the start one in spirit and
one in purpose with a strong desire to serve the
Lord on the mission field some day.

During our senior year, Jim was elected co-
chaplain of our senior class and was responsi-

ble for planning and leading two services each week. As usual, Jim took his responsibility very seriously.

"For the first time," he wrote his mother, "I am beginning to feel a burden for my class-mates. This is a burden of joy. I am urging each senior to launch out into the deep ocean of God's grace."

Jim made a commitment to pray by name for every member of our graduating class. In years to come, his prayer list would include the names of more than 3,000 people, all of whom were lifted in prayer before God's throne every month.

The discipline of fasting at noon one day each week was also begun during college days. Each Thursday, Jim and I, along with more than 100 students, found ourselves on our knees around the altar in Hughes Auditorium. Prayer requests from Asbury alumni, pastors, Christian workers and missionaries scattered all over the world were read. Then earnest in-tercession followed. We counted it a joy to have a small part in praying for people we did not know.

One cold February afternoon in 1953, Jim led me across campus to the original Asbury building constructed in 1890. It was no larger than a two-car garage. A picture of Christ hung on the wall in a quiet upper room and an open Bible rested on a small table.

We entered this hallowed spot where in bygone years hundreds of God's messengers had set themselves apart for missionary service. We knelt and I accepted Jim's proposal for marriage and in prayer we promised each other that we would serve the Lord together someday, somewhere.

June 6, 1953, three days before graduation, the Livingstons from Alabama and the DeLays from Florida met on the campus of Asbury College. Their next meeting would be in St. Petersburg, Florida on July 20, our wedding day.

A threefold cord is not easily broken, for where two are closely joined in holy love and fellowship, Christ will by His Spirit come to them and make the third.

5

On to Nyack

Two suitcases, one hat box and one steamer trunk—and Jim and I and friends and family at the Greyhound Bus Station. We were leaving for "up nauth." No time for tears—just hugs and kisses, promises to pray. We were off, bound for Nyack, New York and the Missionary Training Institute.

Jim and I lived in Wilson Hall, a four-story antique clapboard structure known to all as being condemned by the local Nyack Fire Department as "unsafe for residents." The only way the borough authorities would permit married students to occupy this creaky old relic was to rigidly adhere to one special requirement—a fire patrol.

When a job with the college maintenance department was offered, Jim gladly accepted. I found part-time work as a clerk and window dresser at the small but expensive department store and furrier, Ellish of Nyack. With our cupboards equipped with numerous wedding gifts, we had few needs, and we earned enough to feed ourselves and pay our rent and tuition.

The Christian and Missionary Alliance's honor roll of distinguished patriarchs were names familiar to Jim who knew of his Alliance heritage since early childhood—Simpson, Rader, Jaffray, Tozer, Tingley, Snead. For me, these persons and places like Borneo, Irian Jaya and Cambodia were all strange-sounding names from faraway places. However, it did not take long for me to sense the breadth of godliness and Christian experience among the faculty and Alliance leaders. The bold, courageous vision of such men was impossible to miss. Little by little I would learn about the denomination into which I had married.

To be invited to the home of President and Mrs. Thomas Moseley was a particular privilege. We were excited, for they greeted us commoners like we were the most important guests ever to enter their beautiful home. The president's wife loved to lavish sweet hospitality on her guests. And furthermore, she did everything properly—flowers, delicate china cups and plates, well-starched linens and silver serving pieces.

That evening Mrs. Moseley's menu included attractive finger sandwiches of various shapes and flavors, plus small tea cakes. But when I was served, there on that delicate china plate was a giant, man-sized sandwich!

"I knew you were coming directly from work, my dear," she smiled, "and you would not have had your evening meal. This is just for you!"

The time to seriously plan for the two years of home service and eventually the big step to the mission field was finally upon us. Unknown to us at the time, our leaders in the foreign department were about to make a bold decision to send a new wave of missionaries to Indochina's Vietnam to replace the old pioneers who were fast approaching retirement.

All candidates for missionary service in the '50s were asked: "Do you feel called to a specific mission field or will you go wherever we see the need is greatest?" To accept the latter option meant to apply "open" and be willing to go anywhere. Jim and I applied "open," not feeling any particular call to any one continent or tribe. And we waited for our interviews to begin.

For Jim and me, walking the Christian life meant a firm willingness to be different. For both of us this was a willingness to do what our pastor spoke of in one of his sermons: "Any old dead fish can float downstream, but it takes a live one to buck the current and go upstream."

By the end of our Nyack experience, doing, saying and preaching what seemed right, regardless of the consequences, had become a rather firmly set principle for each of us. When a district superintendent in the Midwest learned of Jim's upcoming graduation, he phoned and invited Jim to candidate in a small town in Ohio.

One weekend in April 1956, Jim flew to Cleveland and then took a bus to the farming community of Lido. Hearing about a divisive spirit of bickering and long-held grudges in this church, Jim proceeded to change the message he intended to give. He preached a straight forward, no-punches-pulled message on the absolute necessity for agape, selfless love in the local church body.

That evening, the elderly farmer in whose home Jim had stayed, said, "Son, I like you a lot and appreciated your sermon this morning. But you will never be called to this church because your words were too clear and too plain for our people."

As the time of graduation for the class of 1956 drew near, we continued to trust the Lord for a ministry somewhere. It was a special delight just one week before Jim's graduation to be asked by Rev. T.G. Mangham, district superintendent of the Southeastern District, to help pioneer a new work in Marietta, Georgia. We would follow Jimmy and Deloris Sunda who had just left for missionary service in Irian Jaya.

Our Nyack days were drawing to a close. For almost three years, babies and small children were all around our apartment. Jim and I loved them all. We had taught Sunday school and Bible clubs for other people's children, had babysat for couples who needed time-out, and yet, to be honest, we always felt like outsiders because we had no little ones of our own.

Finally, it was our turn. On May 10, 1956, Stephen Michael Livingston was born just three weeks before graduation. Grandmother DeLay immediately purchased her first plane ticket to visit her first grandbaby, and Pop (my dad) followed a few days later. Daddy Jim had to sleep down the hall on a cot in our kitchen because our bedroom nursery was filled with the new baby, the new mother and the new grandparents.

At graduation three weeks later as the organ played majestically and the honorable, black-robed faculty passed slowly down the aisle, Bob Moseley, one of the faculty members who had been a missionary in Asia, suddenly stepped out of the procession and said to me, "Hey! You gonna raise that kid in Vietnam?"

Two years later the letter came. The foreign department of The Christian and Missionary Alliance was asking if we would consider appointment to the land of Vietnam and be ready to sail October 3, 1958.

We said, "Yes." Our acceptance was a first step into a long and rewarding life of service to the Vietnamese people.

6

Danang, Place of Beginnings

Mrs. Marie Irwin, veteran missionary of over forty years in the Land of the Smaller Dragon, sat at her desk deep in thought. During the past two years, a total of twenty-two new couples and almost a dozen single missionaries had been directed to Vietnam by the foreign department. A good number of these new recruits had been sent to Tourane, the French name for the city of Danang (Daa NAANG) to begin their missionary careers. Now, in addition to her heavy teaching schedule at the Tourane Bible School and weekend ministries to the thirty-three Tin Lanh churches in Quang Nam (Kwang NAM) province, Mrs. Irwin led the entire orientation process for incoming freshmen missionaries. It was to be her "swan song."

To be sent to Danang at such a time as this was a unique blessing for Jim and me. It was here, forty-seven years before, that the Holy Spirit first ordained that the gospel of Jesus Christ be preached in Vietnam. It was here that Franklin and Marie Irwin saw miracles of healings and people delivered from evil spirits by the power of our Lord Jesus Christ. It was here that Good News, or Tin Lanh, as the Church was called by the Vietnamese, had entered Vietnam.

Mrs. Irwin sat listening to the voices of the Vietnamese children coming from the church next door, the mother church for many others that would follow in Central Vietnam. In perfect unison they chanted their memory verses.

"That's good, little friends," said their leader.

This church had been born in the midst of strong opposition in 1911. Now, in 1958, some 300 Tin Lanh churches were lifting high the banner of the Lord Jesus across South Vietnam. By 1975, the year Vietnam fell to communism, the number would reach close to 500. It would be here in Danang, under the shadow of those valiant patriarchs of the cross, that we too would begin our missionary career.

From the start, Jim and I recognized Marie Irwin as one of the great missionaries of our time. Already almost seventy years of age, she was gracious and kind, yet she could be as stern as a drill sergeant. Nearly four years spent in a Japanese internment camp during

World War II had not diminished Marie Irwin's Christlike graces, spiritual beauty or unmatched energy.

"If you want to survive in the Orient," she informed the new missionaries, "it is imperative that you all have a noon rest every day after lunch." Yet Mrs. Irwin did not observe her own mandate. At 1 p.m. each day, one of several Bible school students would come to her house where she taught them to play hymns on a little Japanese pump organ.

We second-wave missionaries felt an almost deferential reverence for the Christlikeness in Franklin and Marie Irwin. They were equally honored and respected by local government officials and village peasants. From the beginning, their ministry had been anointed by the Holy Spirit, and now we young missionaries were the recipients of their wisdom and experience.

In the late '50s, in political circles around the world, there was much speculation as to the future of the Indochina Peninsula as well as all of Southeast Asia. Thinking men pondered a "domino theory," and surmised that it was just a matter of time until that entire area of the world would fall to communism. The sending of this new wave of more than sixty young people to Vietnam, the strategy conceived by the Alliance, flew in the face of the most prevailing trends. War, poverty, crop loss, famine, the presence of foreign troops and internal corruption—all pointed toward inevitable decay and eventual communist control. Some well-meaning advisors, Mrs. Irwin informed us, had even told our leaders at headquarters, "Cut your losses in Vietnam, Laos and Cambodia and get out! Vietnam and the Indochina Peninsula are falling dominos."

She continued.

"We, the old warriors—the Stebbines, the Carlsons, the Jeffreys and Frank and I, are already past retirement age. Vietnam, although considered to be a field of great harvest and blessing, still has thousands and thousands of people yet unreached, hundreds and hundreds of villages still ignorant of Tin Lanh." *But, mused the veteran missionary to herself, such an unprepared bunch these young people seem to be! So individualistic, so opinionated and so inclined to amusement!*

The fast-paced events of the years just passed had indeed caused concern for political and Mission leaders. The French suffered an embarrassing defeat in 1954 with the fall of Dien Bien Phu (Dee-ONG Bee-ONG FOO) and were forced to leave Vietnam. But they left more like the victors than the vanquished, which they were. There were colorful parades and ceremonies full of pomp and circumstance. Speeches were made and medals awarded as the colonial power, France, resident in Indochina for nearly 100 years, pulled up stakes and left.

Then, in marched the victors—the Viet
Minh. Considering the gravity of the situation,
the contrast was ludicrous. The defeated army
left in glory with the sound of the trumpet and
the roar of armored cars, planes and war ves-
sels. The victors, small, thin and gaunt, arrived
dressed in faded black pajamas and, on their
feet, crude sandals made from salvaged rubber
tires. The defeated troops left to the tune of *La
Marseillaise*! The victors arrived accompanied
by only the soft shuffle of their own feet. The
change of power had taken place.

Vietnam was divided at the seventeenth par-
allel: the North under the iron rule of Ho Chi
Minh (Ho Chee MEN) and General Vo
Nguyen Giap (Vaw WI-ung YAP), and the
South under the shaky rule of Emperor Bao
Dai (Ba-AO Die) soon to be followed by the
feudalistic government of Ngo Dinh Diem
(NGO Din YEE-um).

We three Livingstons were assigned to a
small compound about two blocks from the Tin
Lanh Church and the Tourane Bible School.
Ours was a typical Vietnamese house with cement floors, two small bedrooms and an outside kitchen in the back. Vertical bars on the
windows served as protection and, although
not especially aesthetic in appearance, the
house was adequate.

Still, unanswered questions loomed in Mrs.
Irwin's mind: Do they have what it takes to adjust to Vietnamese culture? Do they have the

physical stamina to endure the rigors of life in the Orient? Will they be able to tolerate the heat? Do they have the determination to persist when discouragement comes knocking at their door? Will they bear up under the strain of inevitable misunderstandings and problems with the nationals and their fellow missionaries, or will they become prey to the thousand and one gnawing insects of irritation which attack even the best of God's chosen ones? Will they have the spiritual fiber to face the gathering clouds of war, bloodshed and terrorism that may soon engulf this land? Will they press on and be willing to suffer? Do they have an abiding, unshakable confidence in their calling to plant churches and evangelize Vietnam?

Mrs. Irwin was not looking at the professional qualifications of these young recruits. She was looking for something even more basic than sincere dedication. It was perseverance! Endurance! Here in Danang, this place of beginnings, will these young missionaries last? Yes, they will start, but will they stay? Will these new missionaries be victors or victims?

7

More Than Polite Conversation

January 3, 1959—we had been in Danang exactly four weeks. Our recently hired Vietnamese teacher peddled to our house at 7:30 that first Monday morning, sat down in front of us at our desk, and said, "*Chau Ong* (Chao AAM), *Chau Ba* (Chao BAA), Greetings, sir, Greetings, madam" and language study officially began.

First-term missionaries must exercise discipline if their intention is to be fluent. Jim and I had only one goal during those first few months in Danang: to make the Vietnamese language our passion and priority. This was our first step toward a preaching/teaching ministry.

We studied the assimilation method which uses mimicry, the way a child learns to talk. The teacher speaks; the student repeats.

Teacher speaks; student repeats, over and over, until each vowel and every tone can be spoken perfectly.

Language tests were required of all missionaries. In fact, the status as a senior missionary at the Vietnam annual field conference was not given to any missionary who had not completed the required two-year language course and passed the examinations that come every three to six months.

During those early months in Danang, we were both blessed and concerned with the fact that in just a few months our family would increase by one. The blessed event would coincide with Language Test #2.

It was the intense hot, dry season. Vietnamese children were suffering from huge, boil-like abscesses on their heads. Missionary children were complaining of irritation and infection caused by prickly heat rash. There was no way to keep their chubby little necks dry of perspiration, hence, the reaction. But the worst was yet to come—the mosquito-caused, dreaded dengue fever.

Toward the end of my ninth month, both Jim and Steve became alarmingly sick. Mrs. Irwin warned her charges, "In the past when the French contracted dengue fever, they were sent back to France. So when the fever hits you, go to bed and stay there!"

Despite being very pregnant and most uncomfortable, several times each day I insisted that Jim and Stevie get out of bed and sit on a little camp stool in the bathroom while I poured pail after pail of room-temperature water over them in an all-out effort to reduce the fever. It worked. Their temperatures never did reach the point of triggering a convulsion. That summer nine Vietnamese children in Danang died from dengue.

August 6, 1959, 1:30 a.m. Jim's bout with dengue had depleted his body of all strength.

"Jim, are you awake?" I whispered.

"Uh . . . what's the matter? Are you getting the fever now?"

"No. It's time for the baby."

I watched Jim drag himself out of bed and go next door to wake up Bill and Marnie Mock. Losing no time, Bill peddled his bike down the dark streets to the Bible school compound and the residence of Dale Herendeen, one of the few new missionaries who owned a vehicle. Minutes later, Dale and Bill whisked me off in Dale's Land Rover to the St. Paul Birth Clinic, leaving behind the two pitiful dengue patients, Jim and Stevie. Jim wrote to his parents a few days later:

> It was one of the hardest decisions I have ever had to make, to let Jean go without me. We were afraid of what Mrs. Irwin called "dengue relapse." She had already threatened me saying, "Mr. Livingston, if you get out of that bed, I will send you home!" And she meant back to the States!
>
> So I stayed at our house, but I might as well

have gone. I couldn't sleep at all that night wondering if Jean were all right. I finally just committed everything to the Lord and slept two hours. Charlie Long came by the house at 8 the next morning. His wife EG had been with Jean all night.

"Charlie, sick or not sick, I am not staying here any longer."

We drove to the clinic and I managed to climb the steps to the second floor and went into the room. There, in a crib, was a wee little form. I was so relieved, I just stood there and cried for joy. Then hurriedly I asked about Jean, not even knowing at that point if the baby was a boy or a girl.

"Jean had a difficult delivery!" EG said. But nothing had escaped the eye of our heavenly Father. A Vietnamese army doctor "just happened" to be in town for a meeting and, not having a place to spend the night, had gone to the clinic. He was there when we needed him.

Big brother Steve was especially delighted with Nancy Ellen, his "Vietnamese" sister. Steve reasoned, *Well, she has black hair like a Vietnamese. She can't speak English like the Vietnamese. She cries the way Vietnamese babies cry. Mama got her at the Vietnamese clinic; so surely this must be a Vietnamese baby!*

From the day we brought Nancy home, big brother and little sister played with one another in none but the Vietnamese language. One day our helpers were washing dishes and talking about our new baby.

"Let's give the baby a Vietnamese name," one said to the other.

There was a pause.

"*Kim Hoa! (Kim WA).* Her Vietnamese name will be Kim Hoa (Golden Flower)." Even today, our daughter Nancy is often called by this lovely Vietnamese name.

The second language test was coming up fast. Four weeks after baby Kim Hoa's birth, dengue fever finally caught up with me. Nevertheless, in the middle of the seven-day dengue cycle, I accompanied Jim to Mrs. Irwin's office once again. Would she suspect? If Mrs. Irwin knew that I was running a fever that day, she never let on.

Yes, together we had passed another hurdle in spite of the heat, bouts with dengue and the birth of a baby. Happy and determined to be teachable in all matters related to Asian culture, we found ourselves growing in admiration and love for the Vietnamese people. We were also becoming stronger in our faith because we had been forced into circumstances where the exercise of that faith in our Almighty God was the only thing we could do.

Yes, language learning is definitely more than just polite conversation!

8

A Chasm to Be Bridged

If looks could kill, then without a doubt Jim would have been a goner the first time he attempted to purchase stamps at the Quang Ngai post office. The sun-bronzed Vietnamese peasants glared at him as if to say, "White devil! You have no reason to be here. We feel about you like we felt about the French. Get out! Leave us alone!"

We were on the doorstep of a new decade, the turbulent '60s, when youth began to question all things. King Selfishness and Queen Cynicism began a dark reign over the minds of millions. For Jim and me, the issue was not clouded. From a human perspective, our assignment to plant churches was nearly impossible. Nevertheless, the goal was absolutely clear in our minds.

We were concerned about this vast unreached province of Quang Ngai in Central Vietnam. How does one build a bridge across decades of hatred and animosity toward the white-faced, long-nosed foreigner and the legacy left by the French? No one was there to show us to the comfortable Mission house which had been built only two years earlier by Harold and Agnes Dutton. It was next to the provincial hospital. We would find that after 100 years of French rule in our newly assigned province of 800,000 people, there was not a single doctor.

How does one handle their skepticism of anything new, their superstition, their diseases and their poverty? How does one bring *Tin Lanh,* "good news," to this timeless culture, especially if the ominous predictions our language teacher would soon make were true?

The Vietnam annual field conference was always held at Dalat. The climate in the highlands was a welcome escape from the heat of the central flat lands where daily temperatures ranged in the high 90s to 105 degrees and the humidity level was equally offensive.

The appointment of the allocations committee would be our chief concern as well as the concern of all the "new-wave" missionaries who had completed their language requirements. This committee would recommend where each missionary would be placed and the type of service they would do.

On the final day of Mission business when

our names were read from the list that included the entire missionary staff, the alloca-
tion was "Jim and Jean Livingston, Quang
Ngai province; second year language study and
church planting."

We returned to Danang to pack and say our
goodbyes.

"You are going to Quang Ngai!" our language
teacher repeated, visibly moved. Tears came to
his eyes, a show of emotion rare on the face of
a Vietnamese. He said, "Missionary, if you go
to Quang Ngai you will be excessively sad!
Everyone in that province is a communist!"

All new missionaries sensed that the control
of Vietnam and her political future must soon
result in a life-and-death struggle against the
determined, communist-trained Viet Cong
guerilas and their North Vietnamese allies.
Their aim was to destroy the South Vietnam
government and unite their country. Even
though the United States was giving millions in
aid to the South Vietnamese Catholic government, already ominous signs were appearing.
Missionary Ken Swain was seeing terrorist kill-
ings at Minh Long. Charlie and EG Long were
forced to abandon their first tribal location at
Tra My (Traa MEE) deep in the mountains. A
number of large-scale engagements had been
fought as government forces pressed for the in-
itiative. Travel restrictions had been imposed
on missionaries in some areas. If all people in
Quang Ngai were communist, as our language

teacher had said, how could we be tolerated and how could we gain converts for Jesus Christ, let alone plant churches?

The truth was we had already felt something of the approaching storm. Yet none of the young missionaries could begin to really appreciate the severity of the coming war that would pit the world's best-equipped army against the disciplined, bamboo technology of the Viet Cong and North Vietnamese Army.

That day, as Jim and I were packing everything once again into barrels, he suddenly put down Stevie's tricycle.

"Jean," he said, "we are going to see a gulf far different from the warm, delightful Gulf of Mexico where we swam in our youth. The gulf in Quang Ngai is bigger than our ability to cope. We will not be the bystanders any longer. From now on, we are the involved."

Quang Ngai was a province with strong nationalistic feelings, a province the French never fully controlled. Under the communist rule, at that time called the Viet Minh (Viet MIN), this province produced Phan van Dong (Phang Vang DOM), who was Ho Chi Minh's right-hand man, and who later became prime minister after Ho Chi Minh's death.

In 1954, when Vietnam was divided into two separate nations each with its own regime and government, 900,000 North Vietnamese moved to the South as refugees. Most of these people were Catholic. Also at that same time,

48,000 of Quang Ngai's choicest men left their wives and children and boarded Russian boats and headed for North Vietnam.

"We will be back in three years—this time to take over!" they openly declared. It took them twenty years but they did return—and they did take over.

South of the Seventeenth Parallel, President Ngo Dinh Diem had consolidated power and set up the much dreaded security police. Diem tolerated any corruption that would help the Catholic Church. In open air markets all across the land one could see the boxes of cheese, corn meal, powdered milk and other dry goods being sold openly. Printed on every box or tin in bold letters was: "Gift from the U.S.A. Not to be Sold or Exchanged." But millions of dollars in relief goods were sold everywhere. The profits from these sales were used to finance the president's secret police, to support members of his family who were appointed to government offices and to build scores of huge Catholic churches in rural villages where the people lived only in simple mud and bamboo houses. Ordinary peasants were not blind to these abuses. The misguided president seemed equally blind to the fact that he played into the hands of his enemies—the communists.

President Diem proceeded to appoint Catholic men to all important offices in the provincial centers, the local districts and villages. Naturally, such action was despised by the poor rice peasants of Quang Ngai; for them the Catholic Church originated in France. The local people had been communist-taught to hate any French influence and to hate anyone with a white face. Since the United States supported the Diem government which was profiting from the sale of most, if not all, of the U.S. relief goods, the overwhelming feeling in this province was: "Who needs the West?" It was common for hardy, sun-bronzed peasants to recall with pride, "We beat the French with only our bicycles. Vietnam for the Vietnamese!" Thus Ngo Dinh Diem alienated himself and his government from the people.

Into this scenario our family arrived. No one knew we were coming. No one met us at the train stop. No one showed us to the Mission house, but since there was only one "American house" in the entire town, it was not hard to find.

Attention had to be given to practical matters first. No electricity! A Coleman pressure lantern was our only source of light. The thing produced so much heat that we preferred not to light it until after dark each evening so as not to heat up the house unnecessarily. No electricity meant no fans. Most nights we would lie under the mosquito nets with a wet washcloth in one hand and a leaf fan in the other, mopping sweat and fanning until sleep overtook us.

Now it was time to thank the Lord for the "big white monster," our kerosene refrigerator which made a grand total of two trays of ice in twenty-four hours! "Thank You, Lord, for bougainvillea bushes and periwinkle flowers. Thank You for the majestic beauty of the distant mountains. Thank You, Jesus, for this new assignment. It looks worse than tough. It looks impossible, but we will wade in and we have You!"

What do you do when faced by centuries of spiritual darkness and 800,000 peasants who want nothing to do with a Western gospel? Were we going to be happy in Quang Ngai?

We fell asleep on our bamboo bed listening to the various new sounds of the night—crickets fiddling out their own little tunes, a peddler selling boiled duck eggs (the late-evening snack of the townsfolk), the rustle of the coconut palms outside the window. And softly, from the direction of the distant mountains, we heard the rapid, staccato tapping on a hollow, bamboo gong. It was best that we could not decipher the message of that bamboo that first night. For if we had known, perhaps we would not have slept at all. The rapping on hollow bamboo was a signal that outside, there in the darkness, the Viet Cong stalk. They come threatening, maybe to kidnap a South Vietnamese government sympathizer, maybe to assassinate a village leader or maybe to inflict forced recruiting of the village youth.

"The Viet Cong are out there! They are near our village!" the distant gongs were saying.

But on that first night, we did not understand the language of the bamboo, and we slept well.

9

'Cuz Coconuts Can't Cry

"*Chet! Chet! Chet!* Dead! Dead! Dead!" The anguished wails of a woman's voice pierced the stillness of the night. Jim and I bolted upright out of heavy sleep. The cries came from the hospital next door and needed no discussion. We knew that in Vietnam the front lines of action were anywhere, often unseen but seemingly always present. Our Quang Ngai province was one of the areas of South Vietnam designated most dangerous.

The sobbing from the hospital compound continued. We sat in the stifling darkness and wondered. *No doubt it's some mother or a young wife attending the now lifeless body of a loved one. Will we ever get used to the sounds of war and death in the middle of the night?*

Two strands of barbed wire served as a fence to separate our Mission house from the only hospital in Quang Ngai province. Our neighbor, Nguyen Van Ba (NGWEE-ung Vang Ba), simply filled the gap as hospital administrator and so-called "war surgeon." With a meager three years of training, he did the best he could under very primitive conditions.

There was no electricity in the poorly equipped operating room. The floor of the delivery room was hard-packed dried mud, as were the floors in all the thatched-roofed wards and buildings. One positive was a deep well, but there was no running water throughout the entire compound except during the monsoon season when rainwater ran everywhere, even up to six inches on the legs of some hospital beds. It was to this place next door that the casualties of war were brought during the wee hours of the night—every night!

The tears of that grieving woman would be followed the next morning by a drab green Vietnamese (VN) Army truck slowly leaving the hospital, passing in front of our house and then heading toward the local cemetery. In the rear we would see the yellow, flag-draped box with four uniformed soldiers seated on either side. Farewell to arms for one more Vietnamese youth.

The seemingly endless misery and suffering endured by the innocent and the not-so-innocent in our province grieved us deeply. We thought Jeremiah's cry, "Oh, that my head were a spring of water and my eyes a fountain of tears! I would weep day and night for the slain of my people" (Jeremiah 9:1). We were finding that slowly, steadily, our eyes were growing accustomed to tears as the spectacle of a brutal guerilla/terrorist war mounted all around us.

Villages that would not cooperate with the communist insurgents were burned. Low-level government officials were assassinated, even school teachers and nurses. Sapper charges twisted bridges to useless steel skeletons and mines along roadways blew civilian buses to pieces. So at first our tears were deep inside the mind and soul, but soon we were indeed becoming familiar with hot, salty tears—real tears.

One day a German doctor appeared at our doorstep. Dr. Carl Weiderman was to head up the Medico team, a humanitarian project founded by the former U.S. Navy doctor, the famous Dr. Thomas Dooley.

"I was hoping that you could help us find a good Vietnamese cook," he said. "Well, actually we need someone to do our washing, to do housekeeping, as well as do our cooking and marketing. We have rented a two-story house down the street, but we don't speak Vietnamese and hardly know where to start."

With a burst of enthusiasm at seeing another Westerner, we set about to find local Christians needing employment. We also found interpreters who could speak English, a rare thing in those days of early 1960. The interpreters would translate a description of the patient's physical symptoms from Vietnamese into English for Dr. Weiderman and his helpers to advise and treat. We wondered, *What treatment will they prescribe the first time the patients tell them they are sick because of the "poisonous wind?"* Many common physical problems, including dengue, colds, fevers, viruses and stomachaches, were all attributed to the poisonous wind.

We helped the Medico staff find furniture and gave practical tips which would make life a little less stressful for the new folks on the block. Dr. Weiderman appreciated this practical help.

"When you find people in your village work," he said, "who need urgent medical attention, do not hesitate to bring them to the hospital. They will receive immediate attention."

How do you bridge the chasm of separation between the suspicious peasants and the gospel of Jesus Christ? A few highly trained professionals in the provincial hospital certainly wouldn't hurt!

All spiritual leadership is serious business. To many of the new missionaries during those war years in Vietnam, all Vietnamese in leadership roles seemed to be so very serious and altogether somber and solemn-faced. Not so with the jolly Vietnamese pastor Nguyen Linh. We were greatly encouraged in finding that Linh possessed a vibrant burden for soul-winning. He began at once to assume his share of the responsibility for the bridge building that loomed so large before us—finding a way to span the chasm and get into the hearts and minds of the proud peasants of Quang Ngai. Linh jumped into this task with an energy and happy enthusiasm that characterized his whole nature.

The gospel had entered the province some two decades before, but in 1960 there were only three small Tin Lanh churches with less than 200 people all together, plus a few other believers sprinkled throughout the area. In the following three years we would be amazed to have a part in the birth of five churches. Our joy was supreme as we helped to instruct new believers who numbered over 900.

From the start we had excellent rapport with Pastor and Mrs. Linh. Even with our limited knowledge of Vietnamese, they welcomed our participation in all the regular activities and outreach programs of the Quang Ngai church. Jim and I both preached there once each month. The Vietnamese culture has a way of fitting everyone into his or her own particular place in the pecking order and family structure, in village life and in church life as well. Vietnamese pastors never refer to a woman speaking before a group as "preaching"—only "testifying." Nevertheless, I grew strong in my Vietnamese language skills by teaching at the weekly children's meetings and "testifying" every Sunday during morning worship services in one of the area churches.

The Linhs often accompanied us on visitation in the rural areas of Nghia Hung (Ngeea HUNG). Then, in God's providence, came An Cuong (ANG Kung) and the beginning of a marvelous turning to God in the poverty-bound fishing villages of Binh Son where at least eighty families had taken down their ancestor altars.

An Cuong was a thatched-hut village in the Binh Son district, population about 1,500 peasant fisherfolk stubbornly clinging to the sandy shoreline of the South China Sea. An Cuong—where people suffered from multiple ailments related to filth and the absence of sanitation. An Cuong—where fresh water was scarce because there was only one village well to be shared by everyone. An Cuong—where the incidence of eye disease was horrific. An Cuong—where everyone was poor and the children experienced the reality of hunger pains because for some reason the fishing beds in the waters along their coastline had vanished, and with them their only cash crop, fish. Thus, the livelihood of most villagers had been reduced to where they had no money for rice. Families just ate dried tapioca root and small shiners, and waited for better times to come.

This was An Cuong. It all began like this.

One Saturday afternoon in August 1960, two elementary teachers from An Cuong appeared at our house. Nguyen Van Tri (NGWEE-ung Vang TREE) and Huynh Sy Hung (When She HUM) had peddled forty kilometers into Quang Ngai town to ask that we come to preach in their village.

"You must come and see, missionary!" they repeated with increasing persuasion.

Little did we know that God had chosen these two young men to be His ambassadors to spearhead a movement that in the next three years would see almost 1,000 people along this coastline abandon their ancestor altars and find a place of hope in the Lord Jesus Christ.

Tri and Hung were themselves only recent converts, saved one night during an outdoor evangelistic meeting at Chau O. These two Vietnamese teachers were so excited that, after their decision to follow Christ, they returned to An Cuong and gossiped the gospel with everyone they met:

> The Great God of the heavens is a God of love. He created man and all the living creatures. Listen up! Listen, friends, listen how we have been deceived for centuries by evil spirits. Man chose to disobey God and to obey the evil spirits. This is sin.
>
> Fellow countrymen, our people are guilty of sin. Listen! We light incense to appease spirits; we avoid business on certain days so as not to evoke

the wrath of evil spirits. We paint big slanted eyes on our fishing boats to see in the dark and avoid the snares of the spirits. We tie amulets on our children's necks to ward off Ong Ke (OM KAY) (the boogie man). Yes, we have always lived in fear of the evil spirits.

As for the Great God of the heavens, this is the One we have neglected! We have drunk heaven's water, eaten heaven's rice and breathed heaven's air. But the most wretched of all our sins is that we have never worshiped the Almighty One from heaven. We have not understood in our blindness that God sent His Son to come to this earth to take on human flesh and make a way to free us from our sins and to put His peace in our hearts. Do you believe this, Tin Lanh? Then what shall we do?

We shall invite the Tin Lanh pastor and the American missionary to come to An Cuong. They will lead us out of our darkness to God.

In August 1960, Jim and our second-year language teacher drove a narrow back road to about two miles from the village and walked in a soaking rain to An Cuong.

Meeting in the thatched-roof schoolhouse, the new babes in Christ prayed together and studied from God's Book. Their peace was real; their joy was contagious. Led by a very intense young student pastor, a young man fully anointed by God's Spirit, Pastor Ngo Thai Binh, the work prospered. The good news, fanned like a flame by the Holy Spirit Himself, blazed from An Cuong village up the beach to a second fishing village, on to a third village and then southward. Satan's anger and hostility showed its ugly face at once. The birth and planting of new churches never goes uncontested.

Small-time local officials became insanely jealous of the large numbers of new believers and the rapid spread of the good news. Force and intimidation were the means they used in attempting to persuade our people to divorce themselves from the Tin Lanh and become Catholics. In December 1960, only six months after our work began in this province, we had locked horns with the enemy.

In an interrogation time with local officials, one of the Christians mentioned Jim, using his Vietnamese name, Le Vinh Ton (LAY Vin Tone). He told of Jim's recent involvement with the new Christians at An Cuong and vicinity. In rage, the official stormed, "If I get my hands on that missionary, I will chop him up and make fish soup out of him!"

Biased as they were against Protestant Christians, it should be said that many of these same Roman Catholic officials were bold and courageous in risking their lives in their desperate struggle against the communist enemy.

It was the Catholic officials who launched the government's Strategic Hamlet Program which had as its goal to hinder the free movement of the communists at night. Each village or hamlet was surrounded with a seven-foot-high bamboo fence. Alongside the fence was an eight-foot-deep trench filled with thousands of spiked bamboo, all facing out. The deep moats, the spikes, the bamboo fences and the miles and miles of barbed wire were supposed to keep the Viet Cong (VC) from coming into a village, taking rice and supplies and persuading the youth to go back with them into the mountains.

In theory, the plan was good. The problem was that sympathizers inside the hamlet would drag open the barbed wire barriers at the entrance of the village during the night. Thus, the VC could easily enter with little or no resistance and then proceed to recruit, to kill and to terrorize the peasants at will.

Because of their open stand against communism, village officials all across our province were targets of the VC guerilla terrorists. Every visit to our home by Christians brought stories of village leaders, nurses and school teachers who were taken captive by the VC and, in front of their families, tied to bamboo poles and executed in cold blood.

And, of course, some of the those victims were brought by stretcher to the provincial hospital next to our home. It was for these poor souls that women cried, "Dead! Dead!" and shed tears in the middle of the night.

The peoples of Asia have an expression: "Coconuts can't cry!" Through these times, when our people suffered persecution and stumbled under the yoke of poverty and affliction, God's best gift to our family was a genuine and enduring compassion for the Vietnamese people. He taught us other lessons too: that love is not merely an emotion, but a thing of the will, and that sometimes means weariness. This weariness, sorrow and tears became an accepted part of daily service.

At the same time, God opened an entrance into villages that for centuries had lived in spiritual darkness. He showed us that even in the presence of abject poverty and all kinds of difficulties, nothing could compare to the matchless glory and blessedness of seeing churches born in these villages.

We wanted to be a family with an honest, genuine, tender concern for our adopted people. We wanted to be missionaries with heart, with feeling, with sympathy. This was our privilege and our responsibility—to weep with those who wept in the night because, after all, coconuts can't cry.

But God's servants can and should.

10

Interruptions

F ew of our friends ever realized that one of Jim's hardest battles has been his own impatient spirit. He once said to me, "Jean, I have a rather constant, youthful and at times unnatural idealism, propelled along by a prophet's heart. But all too often there is a hidden, simmering impatience."

These words of self-evaluation, in my opinion, were rather accurate. Surely God would not call an impatient person to be a missionary, to send that one to a place where patience is a vital virtue. Our first four months at Quang Ngai became a craggy training ground for receiving more of the needed gift of patience.

An upcoming village Bible school was uppermost in our thinking. Working in a language that was several thousand years old, a language so difficult that it required an unbelievable amount of time in the preparation of messages and the oral practice of the same, Jim and I both felt the pressure of our schedules. Before we would be ready to teach new believers in Nghia Hung next week, we needed a large block of uninterrupted time for preparation. It was during that week that lessons on patience came in the form of numerous interruptions, often announced by Dog Toto's barking at the door.

"Wonder who that is?" I asked the children as Toto barked in the driveway.

"It's probably Ol' Beggar Man," I said, answering my own question. This dirty, unkempt fellow, ravaged with venereal disease and who for some reason could not speak, shuffled into our yard often when we first moved to Quang Ngai. Kim Hoa always ran and hid in the kitchen when he appeared. He was harmless, but frightening both in appearance and aroma.

I remembered the day. We did not have any bread to give the poor soul, so we just gave him an egg. In return, he scowled, then cracked off the tip of the egg shell, raised it to his lips and downed the whole thing raw.

"Excuse please, sir, guests have arrived," our helper announced at Jim's door. It was two young men from Duc Pho (DUCK Fo) who had decided this would be a good day to visit the missionary. Chin and Hoa took advantage of perhaps the only benefit they had from working for the Vietnam railway—they hitched a ride to Quang Ngai by train.

Chin and Hoa were train guards who, along

with thirty other soldiers, rode the armored cars every day from early morning to mid-afternoon. Their job: to protect the railway!

"How's it going, friends?" Jim asked.

"Like chewing rocks!" was Hoa's immediate reply. "Everyone knows this is the most dangerous line in the world, and it's getting worse. We are a target for ambush every day."

"Our job," continued Chin, "is to keep watch through the porthole of the armored car. I keep a finger on the trigger of my automatic rifle all the time. Still we get ambushed!"

Jim has many talents as a missionary. One of them is just listening. But sometimes listening can go on and on ad infinitum. The boys seemed pleased to have an audience and told story after story of their encounters with the communists who had infiltrated the province during the past year. Jim shifted his position several times as the stories dragged on and on.

"Are you ever afraid?" Jim finally asked.

"Afraid? We're scared all the time!" came an instant reply.

Then my husband did the thing he loves doing best. He steered the conversation from tales of fear and death to the love and mercy of the Great God of the Skies.

"He is the One who grants peace, a heavenly, forever kind of peace," Jim told them. The soldiers listened with genuine interest.

As Chin and Hoa finally rose to leave, Jim gave them some Tin Lanh tracts explaining

God's simple plan of salvation. He told them to take this literature and give one tract to each of the men in their unit when they returned to the rails the following day.

The dog always barked when visitors—even white-faced ones—came. Our mission home had become a virtual expatriate stopover. Every week missionaries going up and down central Vietnam's coast were our guests for meals and overnight. Even the American consul from Hue stopped by en route to Saigon on official business. We believed that hospitality and Christianity went together well.

Dr. Herb Billman, the eye surgeon from Danang, was with us regularly. He had been flatly denied permission by the Vietnamese surgeons in Danang to perform his "free" surgery. But in rural Quang Ngai, Dr. Billman's professional services were welcomed. Thus Herb became one of our regular house guests and news of his charity ministry of eye surgery to poor peasants spread like wildfire throughout Quang Ngai province.

One particular morning Jim was up before 5 o'clock praying and waiting for enough daylight to read his Bible. This practice, along with the discipline of fasting, were exercises which would intensify in the years ahead.

Today was to be a cloudy one. Good! We needed a good day like this for uninterrupted hard work so as to be ready for the village Bible school next week. There were lessons to finish and charts to be drawn. We needed to check out the equipment . . . and then . . .

"Pastor Ngoc (NGOP) from Duc Pho is here," came the voice of the helper once again.

Jim rose from his papers to greet our pastor friend.

"How is Mrs. Ngoc? How are your children? Did you have good attendance at the services on Sunday?" Jim asked patiently.

"Yes, but one of our Christians was taken by the security police and has been beaten for three days now. We do not know why."

"What about your church secretary, Mr. Tu (TOO)?" Jim was interested in this man who served as a village official at Duc Pho. A Protestant holding a district office was rare!

"He is still in hiding. He comes to church regularly and he goes to the district office each morning, but no one knows where he is at night. He told me he often sleeps in a dry rice paddy since receiving those death threats from the VC. Every night it's a different place. His family says that some day the VC are going to get him."

Mr. Tu was a gentle person whose life glowed with honest Christian virtues. He, along with thousands of other local officials, was a target for the Viet Cong. Because his life had been threatened, Mr. Tu would not risk his family's security by sleeping at home. A water buffalo shed or a rice paddy became his bedroom.

This brave man also carried the burden of the

Duc Pho church building program as well. He and Pastor Ngoc were seeking ways to raise money for this project.

"How much will you give me for my bicycle? It is in good condition. See, the gears work well. Give me a good price!" Mr. Tu had sold his bicycle—the equivalent in our country of someone selling his only car—to give the entire amount toward the church building fund. He had been doing without wheels ever since. A man who sleeps in a rice paddy does not need a bicycle.

A few minutes later, Pastor Ngoc left. Jim glanced at his watch.

"Interruptions!" he blurted. He felt an immediate check in his spirit.

The afternoon proved to be a carbon copy of the morning. Pastor Linh came to make final plans for the Bible school.

Now it was supper time. It had been a day of nonstop interruptions. The sky was becoming dark when Dog Toto's loud barking caused us to look up from the supper table. Into our yard came a black-pajamed peasant soaked to the skin from the drizzling rain. He was leading a young girl about fourteen years old.

Jim excused himself.

"Oh, missionary, Doctor told me he could do nothing for my daughter Mai," Anh Dinh (Unh DIN) said. "Doctor told me to bring her to the hospital five months ago, but I couldn't."

"Why, Anh Dinh, why did you wait so long?" Jim asked, trying not to show his exasperation. These seashore villagers were skeptical of anything unknown and would often refuse to leave home even for medical help.

"Missionary, you know we are terribly poor," came the reply. "The ocean does not give much fish these days. I had no money for *lambretta* (bus) fare. It is hard for us to come this far. Now, Mai can hardly see. Look at her, Missionary. See for yourself. But we're here now. Why doesn't Doctor help her? Oh, Missionary! You talk to Doctor."

Actually, it was only about forty kilometers from An Cuong to our house, but to these simple fisherfolk it was like traveling halfway around the world. And to people who have no money for even their daily rice, the cost of this short journey seemed next to impossible.

Jim returned to the table to ask Dr. Billman about the girl.

"I cannot improve her sight. They waited too long," he finally said.

How do you tell a father that there is little or no hope that his daughter will ever see clearly again? His child, who two years ago was seeing normally, was nearly blind and beyond the help of the best surgery.

"She has very high pressure inside the eye. An operation would be risky at best. In the next five months if the pressure continues to increase, I will operate. But an operation now might result in complete blindness. I would rather wait."

Some missionary work is not without sorrow of heart. There are times when you weep openly; at other times, you just weep deep in your heart. This was one of those occasions.

Jim and Herb sat and talked after our two unexpected Vietnamese guests had retired for the night.

"Herb," Jim said finally, "I am deeply burdened for sick people who come to our house week after week. The serious cases we take to the Medico doctor, but there are hundreds of ailments still needing attention out in the village that we could help prevent if . . . if . . . Herb, would you would be willing to accompany us to the seaside villages sometime?"

Herb agreed to go with us the following month.

Each day the rest of that week Dog Toto continued to faithfully announce the arrival of visitors, and between interruptions, the missionaries grabbed odd moments here and there to finish preparations for the village adult Bible school.

The first morning as I was teaching, a mortar screamed in from the east, whizzing over the church and making a direct hit just west of the building. We did not know whether to duck, hit the floor or continue on as if nothing had happened. We did the latter.

The Bible school at Nghia Hung proved to

be God's strategy for strengthening new believers to stand true in times of trouble. It was the forerunner of succeeding village Bible schools in our province. District superintendent Vong later commented, "I would like to see every province have such a school."

The Bible schools were narrowing the gap between the gospel and the suspicious peasants of Quang Ngai province.

11

Spy at My Table

"Anything, anywhere!" That is what I had told the Lord years before, but of course I meant that I would be willing to do all those adventurous things that missionaries might do—like traveling through tiger country! But teaching English? No! That was definitely not high on my list of sparkling missionary activities!

The two neatly dressed Vietnamese merchants had arrived unannounced. They stated their purpose almost immediately.

"Ma'm, we want you to teach us English."

"Well, er . . . , " I was stalling.

I recognized the men immediately. Mr. Vinh (VIN) was a tailor on Main Street in our little town. His friend Ban (BANG) was a handsome bachelor and the owner of a variety store. Two-year-old Kim Hoa was already acquainted with Ban and his lovely sisters. They often coaxed her into their shop by promising to give her sweets.

Why did Ban and Vinh want to study English? U.S. Army advisors had just arrived in Quang Ngai. Suddenly studying English became the latest indoor sport with ambitious Vietnamese all over town. Local merchants wanted to bid for the services that the 170 Americans might need on their compound. Vietnamese women wanted jobs washing and ironing uniforms. We surmised that Vinh and Ban were out to get their piece of the pie as well.

In an effort to convince me to become their teacher, the determined shopkeepers then proposed that they would pay me for my services. With some reluctance I agreed to teach just one afternoon a week, but I told them that the money which they paid me would not be for personal use but to purchase medicines for the poor that lived in our fishing villages.

Little by little the three of us became better acquainted. It never occurred to Jim and me that behind their struggles with phonics there lurked a far darker motivation for studying English.

But first I must tell you about the way the Spirit of God was moving in our province.

In June of 1960 when we arrived in Quang Ngai province there were only three pastors shepherding three small churches among more than 800,000 unevangelized people. Jim and these three young Vietnamese pastors determined that regardless of the opposition and the pervasive communist guerilla presence in the province, they would enter every village that seemed to offer an opening.

Behind each of these evangelistic endeavors would be regular times of prayer and fasting. It was our belief that God's divine blessing would come first and foremost through the local church. Our task was to do all we could to make this happen.

Who can explain the reason why over 600 fisherfolk accepted Christ in the village of An Cuong? Why did another 245 accept Christ at Phuoc Thien, 40 more at Binh Duc and 69 more at Nghia Hung? How was it possible that at Nghia Hung, Mo Duc, Chao O, An Cuong, Phuoc Thien and Le Thuy—villages all struggling with extreme poverty—in spite of persecution and harassment from district officers, and in the face of unending VC terrorist activity, hundreds of one-time communist-inclined peasants came to accept Jesus Christ as Savior, entered newly planted churches and in their joyful newborn enthusiam built five church buildings?

One decisive reason was our firm resolve to outdo the communists in using the power of the printed page. The Tin Lanh Press in Saigon had printed some superb twenty- to forty-page palm-sized booklets and gospel tracts. Over several years, more than 300,000 pieces of literature would be distributed. Everywhere we went peasants would rise up from their work in the fields and, extending dirt-soiled hands, wave to us in hope of receiving a piece of reading material.

From the start, the fisherfolk in the villages were excited about finding Jesus as Savior. Only a few kilometers apart, most folks usually took the shortcut to visit from village to village by simply walking up or down the beach. These new believers were the Holy Spirit's key instruments in gossiping the gospel. Active faith is a contagious thing, and in each place new Christians had a willingness to share their newfound faith and thus prepare the way for *bo dao* (BOW dow).

What is *bo dao*? This is a Vietnamese term which literally means "to announce religious truth." It has come to mean any evangelistic preaching service held in a public place easily accessible to the community. For example, a *bo dao* could be held in a school yard or in front of the local clinic or on a soccer field. *Bo dao* was another one of those beautiful bridges that the Lord used to span the gap between Jesus and the lost in Quang Ngai province.

As the discussion proceeded Jim was thinking, Bo dao *evangelistic preaching is nighttime preaching. What about the hundreds of Viet Cong and North Vietnamese out at night on the prowl? What about late evening travel to and from the preaching site?*

"Missionary, the schedule will be as follows." Pastor Ngo Thai Binh's gold front tooth flashed as he placed steaming cups of tea on the table. In Vietnam one drinks tea before starting to do anything. It gives time for courtesy talk, time to rest after a journey, time for reflection and a way to ease into more serious matters.

At that time Pastor Binh was shepherding three seaside congregations besides his regular charge at Chau O. This morning he was accompanied by the two natural leaders of An Cuong village, Mr. Que (QUAY) and Anh Nhan (An NYUNG). Never had there been a more opposite match. Mr. Que had once been a communist leader in the province. He was quiet and everybody's friend. Anh Nhan was a hot-tempered, impulsive sort of fellow. Surprisingly, the two got along beautifully together.

Pastor Binh lost no time in stating the purpose of our up-coming visit to An Cuong.

"After we arrive," he began, "we will take our things to the house of Nhan where you will sleep tonight. Then we will visit house-to-house. Let's go! We can talk on the way."

Leaving Highway 1 we traveled eighteen kilometers to An Cuong and Pastor Binh continued outlining the strategy for the upcoming *bo dao*.

"Now, I have a list of at least twenty families who are ready to pray," smiled the young pastor. "But first we will visit Sister Duong (YOU-ung) whose baby is sick."

The path leading to Sister Duong's thatched-roof hut was rocky and narrow. Perhaps fifty or more dirty, screaming children followed us, pushing, shoving, all wanting to get a better glimpse of or even touch the tall Americans.

"Oh, this American man, he's so tall!" said one little kid. "Look, even his nose is tall!"

Jim and I bent low to enter the dark, smoke-scented dwelling. At An Cuong doorways were built for Asian-sized people, not lanky Americans.

The poverty of these people never ceased to disturb us. Pastor motioned toward the thick wooden planks resting on two sawhorses and invited us to sit down. This bed was the only piece of furniture in the room—no table, no chairs, no curtains, no decorations whatsoever, just this big plank bed and a hammock swinging back and forth with a tiny form cupped inside. A somber photograph of President Ngo Dinh Diem hung high on the unpainted, mud-packed wall. The president's face stared out into space totally unaware of the plight of this woman and her baby.

It seemed to Jim and me that the scene in this humble, one-room hovel represented a microcosm of the nation's ills: an aloof president whose sole aim was to cling to his power and advance the Catholic Church, a man who looked the other way while thousands of his people were destitute, diseased and hungry.

"Greetings, older sister," the pastor said. "We have come to pray for your baby."

Sister Duong lifted the child from the hammock. The day was stifling, but the baby, burning with fever, was wrapped tightly in filthy black rags.

"It is probably the poisonous wind that has made my little one so sick," moaned Sister Duong. "I don't want to lose this one."

How does one pray for divine intervention knowing that ninety-five percent of the sicknesses at An Cuong are caused by insufficient diet, poor sanitation, terrible hygiene, nasty habits, lack of water and just plain filth?

For this reason we had chosen to leave our precious Kim Hoa at home with our Vietnamese helpers. I once saw a baby die from dysentery in only four days! With the scarcity of well water, these fishing villages were foul beyond description, and the concept of washing hands before eating was absolutely foreign. The result was a high prevalence of trachoma, tuberculosis, impetigo, boils, scabies and even yaws. Kim Hoa would be best left in the loving care of our helpers until she was a little older.

Sister Duong's baby whimpered when we laid our hands on its little body. We prayed and committed both baby and mother to the mercy of our Lord. I gave the mother instructions to crush half an aspirin in water and give it to the baby. We also suggested that she bathe the baby's face and hands to help bring down the fever, but we knew that our advice would go unheeded. Ignorance and superstition were the mocking angels of death in these villages.

Mr. Que and Anh Nhan led us on to the next home. They explained to us how Uncle Sang had been told about Jesus Christ by his brother-in-law and he had seen the joy and peace which Thuan was experiencing. When he pulled down his ancestor altar, no bad luck followed. Plus, one could not deny that the skin sores which had been such an irritation to Thuan were now totally gone.

"The Lord Jesus does miracles!" Jim said aloud.

"Sang, are you ready to give up worshiping the spirits of your ancestors and accept Christ as your Savior?" Pastor Binh asked.

"I am ready," came Sang's response as he respectfully folded his arms over his chest and prayed. We knew that his decision might well mean being jailed by the district Catholic officials. We also knew that Sang would share all that he learned with his wife and children and they too would accept Christ.

This was the pattern that the Holy Spirit used. In the early phase of village work, the inquirer was led to receive Christ in his own home with perhaps several dozen onlookers at the windows and open door. The second public witness of his new faith would take place six months later at the time of his water baptism.

Still, there was the legitimate need to introduce Tin Lanh to the entire village in a more official way. The *bo dao* was the answer. News of this special meeting would be announced by battery-operated megaphone, the job Stevie liked best. Who could imagine that a five-year-old, Vietnamese-speaking, American boy riding in the back of a Land Rover could be calling a village steeped in centuries of darkness, a village which sheltered numerous trained terrorists, to a night of *bo dao*?

At the meeting place, loudspeakers are placed in key spots so that the singing and gospel message can be heard several hundred yards away. And then we wait—wait for the fishermen to come in from the ocean, wait for them to have their baths by the one and only village well, wait for them to eat rice and wait for them to come to the *bo dao*.

The moon rises over the South China Sea like a big yellow pumpkin, awesome in appearance. The breeze from the ocean is a welcome change from the torrid heat of the day. About 8:30 a crowd begins to gather, a sea of several hundred faces, many folks squatting on the ground near the front, others standing on the fringes, each a precious, living soul.

The microphones squawk and squeal as someone attempts to adjust the volume button on the battery box. Pastor Binh gives the welcome followed by special music, and then a vibrant message meant to persuade listeners that Jesus Christ is God Himself in human flesh, that the God of the heavens has the power to deliver man from evil powers, to forgive sins and to grant to His followers a new life in His Son.

Then, the climax, the call, an invitation for the people of An Cuong to accept Jesus Christ as their personal Savior. Some weary mothers pick up their sleeping babes and slip out into the darkness. But most of the crowd lingers on. Then one by one they come to the front—dark sun-bronzed faces etched with the cares of life. They come, heads bowed, arms folded, maybe six, maybe ten, maybe twenty.

Pastor Binh raises his arms as if to embrace them all and then leads the circle of inquirers in the sinner's prayer. Each one repeats the prayer, word by word, sentence by sentence. And in the wings, Jim and I are praying that the Holy Spirit will defeat the forces of evil and bring victory in Jesus' name. Pastor Binh is pleased. At this village beside the South China Sea, a different kind of fishnet has been drawn to the shore. Oh, the joy of the catch!

After a year the combined body of believers at An Cuong and Phuoc Thien has reached almost 500. Two needs become apparent: a full time pastor and two church buildings.

Rev. and Mrs. Bui Phien (BOOI Fee ang) are called. The people have a heart to build. Yet buildings cost money and money they do not have.

"I pledge two logs," one said.

"I pledge twenty pieces of igneous rock from the hills. My sons and I will cut it ourselves," said another.

"I pledge two bags of cement," promised yet another.

Accompanied only by the melody of waves breaking gently on the seashore, the faith promises are voiced and recorded in the secretary's book. To hear a pledge for so much timber or stone, a pledge for so many kilos of calcimine may sound rather ordinary to the Western ear. But to a people who live in packed-mud houses in a village where there is not even one cement floor or one dwelling with walls made of cement blocks, these pledges are sacrifices too dear to be calculated.

But progress in the kingdom was not without attacks by the evil one who unceasingly contended for his long-held territory in the hearts of these people. He contrived a hundred beguiling harassments.

"Last night, some dirty, low-down scoundrels slipped up to the church property and deliberately smashed over 200 red clay tiles that were meant for the church roof!" the hot-tempered Nhan stated as they burst into our living room one day.

"Didn't we literally chisel the rock out of the ground ourselves to form the foundation of our church? Didn't our women pound the coral and shells from the sea to make the limestone for the mortar? Didn't God multiply our faith and send help from a church in the States to purchase the red roof tiles? Tomorrow we intended to begin laying the roof and now this happens! Missionary, we are going to find out who did this and then I'm going to take my fist to them; that's what!" blared Nhan.

We were indeed sympathetic, even angry ourselves, but to raise our fists and fight back was not the answer. We tried to console the men and encouraged them to continue the work and trust the Lord. God would provide.

Weeks later, the pain of the broken roof tiles was all but forgotten. The building was completed. Visitors came in droves to see the beautiful new church at An Cuong. The kitchen crew informed us later that they fed rice to over 500 people on the first day and half that many the second day. Following the dedication service, one of our visitors testified, "This place is a true miracle of sacrificial giving."

"But missionary, you know what really gives us joy?" Nhan smiled as the others nodded in agreement. "It is when we are out in our boats at night pulling in the nets. Sometimes we are cold and sleepy, always hungry! We just look back to the shore and there on this little hill above our village is our church with the cross pointing upward to Duc Chua Troi, the Great God of the heavens. And we are warm inside again."

We prayed for God to call young people into the work of His kingdom from this newly planted church. And He did! Four young men with their wives applied and were accepted to study at the Nhatrang Bible School. One of those was Huynh Sy Hung, the elementary teacher and one of the first believers at An Cuong. He continues to serve the Lord today in communist Vietnam. Praise God!

Dr. Herb Billman accompanied us to these villages as he promised. He soon realized how desperate the villagers' living conditions were. He examined hundreds and treated as many as he could. We made appointments for dozens of sick and ailing people to come to the provincial hospital for further treatment or surgery. And, before our enemies who did everything they could to shame the Lord's good name, most villagers had to admit that the Tin Lanh people cared for the total person—body, soul and spirit.

Many times after *bo dao* meetings, we would return home long after midnight and, crawling under the mosquito net, find ourselves too exhausted to even think. A few days later we would hear of an ambush near a certain backroad or a bridge we had just traveled and we would say, "Oh, we were just over that bridge!" We knew the Lord had kept His hand upon our going out and our coming in.

But we were totally shocked when we heard a couple of years later that my English student, whose donations I had accepted to purchase medicine for the poor, this man who was an eyewitness and listening ear to many of our family activities week after week for almost two years, was the treasurer, the fourth-ranking communist officer over Quang Ngai province—the tailor, my student Mr. Vinh. For two years he was my own personal spy sitting across from me at my dining room table.

Jim and I would one day wonder just how we managed to stay alive in war-ravaged Quang Ngai.

We finally concluded that our spy friend Mr. Vinh had passed word down to the insurgents all over the province: "Don't kill the skinny American missionaries. I know them. They are harmless!"

A year later, Vinh was captured and died in the Quang Ngai prison.

12

Oh, Vietnam! Vietnam!

We landed at Saigon's Tan Son Nhut Airport in the summer of 1964, Ramona Joy cradled in my arms. Steve, age eight, and Kim Hoa, age five, trailed along beside us. Coming back for our second term, we were surprised to find that we were not returning to Quang Ngai but that our new assignment was: Jim and Jean Livingston—Youth Ministry, Saigon.

During those years of military escalation, Saigon had become one of the least lovely places one would choose to serve the Lord, much less raise a family. With the war had come barbed wire everywhere and garbage piled high on the streets of the city. There were also the protest demonstrations of dissident Buddhists and even a self-immolation by an angry monk in the street. And with the war had come quick prosperity, corruption, crime and incredible traffic congestion with an influx of private cars—Suzukis, Hondas, Lambrettas, army trucks and jeeps by the thousands. During those days, more than 280,000 motorbikes belched forth what became a daily dome of gray-black smog which hung over Saigon, a cloud which could be seen from a distance of twenty-five miles out in the delta.

Also, with the so-called war prosperity had come promiscuity and the inevitable prostitution. One section of the city near the airport boasted a mile-long street of brothels. The prevailing attitude seemed to be "do what you can to please the Americans and make a fast buck doing it." Little did we know that twenty years down the road we would be working with the offspring of this moral decline as all over the land American GIs slept with Vietnamese women. The result would be a segment of despised humanity, one of the legacies of the war in Vietnam, the Amerasians. But for now we just stood by feeling helpless and watched as many of the respected courtesies of Vietnamese culture were abandoned and replaced by an insatiable greed for the mighty American dollar.

We missed our simple Quang Ngai peasants and wondered if we would ever be happy in Saigon. We had no way of knowing that in Vietnam's crisis hour our disappointment in not returning to Quang Ngai would be turned to joy supreme. How could this be? During the next six years a door of opportunity was opened by God's Spirit to touch the lives of many thousands of desperate, needy South Vietnamese men and youth in service for their nation in ARVN.

However, the new term began with a different ministry. The Christian and Missionary Alliance's beautiful, newly finished, two-story building located one block behind the American Embassy was a combination school for teaching English, a youth center and the International Church of Saigon.

"Jim, I still have a problem with the idea of teaching English," I confided one afternoon on the way to the center. "This just does not seem like real missionary work to me."

"It is all in the way you look at it, Jean. You could moan and say, 'Oh, dear! I have got to teach English tonight.' Or you might smile and say, 'Wow, I give them my one-hour English lesson; then I have the designated twenty minutes to witness for Christ, and this several times a week to hundreds of Vietnamese!' It's a unique way to reach the youth of Saigon, an opportunity we must grasp, especially when it seems that half of Saigon's population want to learn English."

And so they came. Not just youth. More than 550 Vietnamese sons and daughters of merchants, influential government officials and prosperous middle-class adults filled ten classes of various levels. Some had only one desire—to learn English and some day work for Americans and make money. Others were interested for academic, travel and cultural reasons.

The focus of each session was to give a solid hour of English as a Second Language (ESL) instruction and then for twenty minutes present the gospel to every student. Following the structured English lesson, an invitation was given to one and all to return to the youth center on Saturday evening for a message to be preached in English and interpreted into Vietnamese. Our motive was singular: to win Saigon's youth to Christ. To our immense joy, God blessed the program.

Then Ruth Jeffrey phoned. With forty-four years of missionary service in Vietnam, Mrs. Jeffrey was about to lead us into a change of direction. Jim had always looked upon Mrs. Jeffrey's father, Dr. Jonathan Goforth of China, as one of the greatest missionaries of the past century. The reading of his biography had been used by the Holy Spirit to initiate a decisive, abiding call in Jim's heart.

"Garth (Garth and Betty Hunt lived with us on the same compound; our respect for this dedicated couple knew no bounds), could you and the Livingstons meet me at the Cong Hoa Military Hospital this Sunday evening at 6?" she said. "I have permission from the top administrator for some of the wounded Vietnamese soldiers to come to the auditorium. My helper Canh will show a sports film. I am praying that we can get a chance to witness to these boys."

Mrs. Jeffrey was what I call a visionary. And Garth Hunt and Jim and I were to become a part of her vision. She grasped this unusual opportunity to reach another segment of Vietnamese youth—the wounded soldiers at the Republic Military Hospital.

I shall never forget the scene that first evening in the hospital auditorium. Over 200 noisy and curiously bandaged men wearing loose-fitting, faded blue pajamas were seated before this little white-haired lady vigorously pumping away on a portable organ. You could not hear the music for the noise. Mrs. Jeffrey looked up as we entered the auditorium, quite obviously relieved that we had arrived.

"Oh, Garth, Jim, finally! Here! I am turning it over to you now."

Seated before us that first night were men from every province in Vietnam. They all had two things in common: One, they had fought to defend their country from the communists; and two, they were all sick or wounded. Now at this military hospital, they waited, some to be discharged with a grossly disfigured body, but most to mend and return to the battle zones.

I stared at the audience. Before us were soldier boys with heavy leg casts, some with chest and arm casts, some amputees and some whose swollen heads were wrapped in multi-layered gauze. Dozens of men seated before us had skin blotched with the pockmarks made by shrapnel. Eyes gazed at us from behind faces forever stretched out of shape, warped by angry burns. And there were the ones with no visible wounds who milled about with a strange, spaced-out look in their eyes, the victims of traumatic battle stress.

I looked aghast at one soldier. Where his nose should have been, there was a tubular piece of flabby skin looking like an elephant trunk extending down from his nasal cavity and attached to his chest. I later realized he was in the long process of cosmetic rehabilitation. He was getting a new nose.

Almost every time we met with these men our service was interrupted by the clackety-thud of an incoming chopper. We knew what that sound meant—men on stretchers lying in pools of their own blood—a sight forever etched in our minds.

That first night, our informal program was hardly more than an attempt to introduce ourselves and give a brief witness about the Holy God who gave His Son Jesus Christ to redeem a sin-sick and suffering world. We simply were not prepared emotionally for this room full of wounded humanity. But we promised to return the following Sunday night and at that time there would be a proper program with singing and a message of encouragement and hope.

The army of pajama-clad wounded cheered and clapped enthusiastically. This was our welcome back for future Sunday evenings and a hospital evangelistic ministry that would continue for the next eight years.

We had been working with the Vietnamese Armed Forces for two years, but our former ministry in Quang Ngai province was never far from our hearts. One day we received news which evoked smothered sobs. Our friends, the lay leaders at An Cuong, Mr. Que, the former communist official, and Anh Nhan, had both been brutally killed by the communists—shot to death in front of their families and fellow Christians. We wept.

I thought back to the time I had sent Mrs. Que some vitamins. She was weak and suffering from dizziness. Later when we visited, the baby had already been born. I could still hear Mr. Que's gentle voice inviting me to name their new baby girl.

"All right, Mr. Que," I had said, lifting the little one wearing only a tiny black shirt.

"I will call this little baby Phuoc (FOOK), meaning 'Blessing.' You and Mrs. Que, you are a blessing to my husband and me. And you have been a blessing to hundreds of people in this fishing village. Yes, Blessing is a good name for your new baby."

Little Miss Blessing was brought and dedicated to the Lord on the very first Sunday the

Christians met in their beautiful new building overlooking the South China Sea.

And Anh Nhan. How he had loved Stevie and Kim Hoa! Each time we went to An Cuong he would take them swimming in the sea. And now Anh Nhan was gone too, leaving a wife and several children with no one to fish the sea and support them any longer.

But still more sad news came. Marines had defeated the enemy north of our Quang Ngai home along the Binh Son coast. In the struggle they swept in a circular movement and trapped and killed 600 VC and NVA. But many of our Binh Son Christians from the villages of Le Thuy and An Cuong lost their lives in the crossfire of the battles.

A few days later, we received still another letter. The communists had taken our An Cuong church building and had been using it as a classroom to teach their devilish doctrine. So when the U.S. Navy gunmen off shore detected enemy fire coming from the largest and most visible structure in the village, they naturally returned fire toward the communist-held structure. The blast that leveled the building destroyed our Tin Lanh church!

Oh, Vietnam! Vietnam! We weep for the Smaller Dragon.

13

To the Armed Forces

"Jim, look at you. You haven't got a dry thread on you!" I scolded with a smile. Missionaries in Asia combat the heat twelve months of the year, but Jim's clothes were more than sweaty that afternoon.

"What happened?" I inquired.

"Oh, sweetheart, it was great!" Jim began. "Our team was standing outside and got soaked to the skin in a tropical downpour. But when the rain stopped, we preached and gave out 200 copies of the Gospel of Luke to the new recruits as they stood high and dry under the eves of a building. After that, we drove over near the assembly ground where we preached again to over 1,000 men. And everywhere we went, the reception was fantastic! These boys are anxious for something to read and we have just what they need!"

The story of a typical Vietnamese soldier begins at basic training camp. During the peak of the war, in our area alone, anywhere from 300 to 1,000 young men were brought each week to the Quang Trung (Kwang TRUM) Military Training Center. The same numbers completed their training course and marched out to war. Within this sprawling complex were facilities to house and train 23,000 men.

"The typical boy at Quang Trung is extremely shaken when he is caught up off the streets of Saigon," Jim explained to our most recent visitor, Jack Falkenberg, president of Bible Literature International (BLI).

"Are the men drafted or what?" asked Jack.

Jim chuckled, but the truth was that the draft in Vietnam was no laughing matter.

"Well," continued Jim, "perhaps a young student is walking home one evening, or maybe he is riding his bicycle home from an English class. Suddenly he hears the shrill sound of a police whistle. An army truck pulls up alongside. Several armed soldiers hop down from the back of the truck.

" 'Let me see your ID card,' demands the officer in charge. If the young man is the right age for the current draft requirements, he is immediately hustled off to the nearest precinct. After six days of so-called processing, the lad finds himself with a dog tag hanging from his neck. This is the draft—Vietnamese style."

Our friend Jack was getting a new slant on

the war in Vietnam, one which had not reached U.S. newspapers. Jim continued.

"The young recruit may have never slept a night in his life without a mosquito net, but for the next twelve weeks he marches, drills, runs, fires and cleans various weapons, and listens to seemingly endless lectures from 5 each morning till sunset. Bone weary by 9 o'clock, the boy doesn't even notice he has no mosquito net. He is a soldier now, and his new address is Quang Trung Military Training Center."

"I'm impressed, Jim. What can BLI do to help?" offered Mr. Falkenberg.

"Literature!" came the immediate reply. "This month alone we have distributed 8,000 copies of our illustrated magazine *Rang Dong* (*The Dawn*). I could have used 40,000!"

"You've got them!" the visitor replied.

In miltary camps up and down the land God gave entrance into the hearts of thousands of soldier boys. These young men, so fearful of the future, never scoffed at our witness. On the contrary, Jim, Garth Hunt, LeRoy Josephsen in Danang and our Vietnamese team were always greeted by smiling faces. One would think their father or older brother had come to visit them.

In addition to the assistance of Bible Literature International, we were also grateful for the help of the Gideons who supplied us with thousands of Vietnamese New Testaments for distribution to the troops in camps, military prisons and on lonely and dangerous firebases all over South Vietnam. Their timely help, as well as that from the Pocket Testament League, which furnished several million Gospel of John portions, helped us to get God's Word into the outstretched hands of a war-ravaged population. Bible Literature Interational also covered the cost of printing the *Rang Dong* magazine every month for nine years. BLI's budget for the Vietnamese military ministry in 1968 alone was $36,000. Our Alliance missionaries, Royce and Betty Rexilius, coordinated the production of much of this quality literature.

Another important visitor to Saigon in the mid '60s was Dr. Bob Pierce, veteran missionary to Korea and founder of World Vision. We took Dr. Bob to our Cong Hoa Hospital Sunday evening rally. After the service, Garth Hunt approached him.

"Dr. Pierce, you witnessed thirty-one boys seeking Jesus tonight. Now Jim, my wife Betty and our team will visit their bedsides to explain the plan of salvation and pray the sinner's prayer again with each one just to make sure they really understand. Most often we will find five or more of their buddies gathered around the bed ready to confess their sins and seek Christ as well."

Garth continued. "Dr. Bob, we missionaries want to be a comfort to those who have looked into the eyes of death. At this time there is no place in all Vietnam where men are turning to

Christ as they are here at this military hospital. Every week anywhere from thirty-five to seventy wounded soldier boys reach out to accept Him."

"What can I do to help?" came Pierce's quick response.

"We need wheelchairs and crutches, Dr. Bob. Because of the nature of this war in which the VC plant land mines and booby traps everywhere, there are thousands of serious leg wounds and hundreds of leg amputees. The Vietnamese government has no funds for wheelchairs and has provided only a limited number of crutches. These men are desperate for this equipment."

Thus World Vision came sweeping into Vietnam, and in the succeeding years furnished over 3,000 wheelchairs for amputees and paraplegics and aluminum crutches too numerous to count for single-leg amputees.

President Lyndon Johnson promised to transport as many relief goods as World Vision could muster. He kept his word. Tons of goods started arriving and the keys to the World Vision warehouse were placed in the hands of missionaries Garth Hunt and Jim Livingston.

In resettlement villages, where a thousand or more war widows had been shifted, we handed out sewing kits, vitamins, kerosene stoves and children's clothing. To the Vietnamese troops in the battle zones we distributed hygiene kits with soap, towel, body powder, toothbrush,

toothpaste, comb, mirror and always copies of
the Word of God and quality Tin Lanh tracts.

At the primary school attended by the children of paratroopers and special forces volunteers, we distributed kits of crayons, scissors,
paper, ruler and pencils—all gifts of love from
Christians in America.

One day we received a letter from Katherine
Kuhlman. It arrived in response to a letter Jim
had written telling her about our work with the
military and our need for a Christian Vietnamese servicemen's chapel in Saigon. In just three
weeks she responded with a check for $20,000.
This marked the beginning of Miss Kuhlman's
generous support which included financing a
special hospital for Vietnamese rangers, training nurses to work with quadriplegics and
equipping a rehabilitation unit of the Cong
Hoa Hospital—all of it done in the name of Jesus Christ.

For us missionaries, these gifts from various
organizations were a means to an end. They
opened doors of opportunity to share Christ
with the Vietnamese military. At each place we
stood before hundreds, sometimes thousands,
of serious listeners and shared Tin Lanh, the
good news. Everyone present was given a copy
of the Gospel of John and a piece of literature
furnished by our Alliance Press.

It was Thanksgiving Day, 1966, but we did
not celebrate in the traditional way. Steve and

his dad spent most of the day in the field with the chief of the Hoc Mon (Hop MONG) district. Late Thanksgiving afternoon, the two of them, along with Kim Hoa and Mona, visited me at the birth clinic where baby Tara Suzanne had just been born.

"Sorry, Mom," blurted twelve-year-old Steve sheepishly. "The soldiers had an American Thanksgiving dinner, and we filled a plate for you—cranberry sauce and everything! But . . . er . . . we forgot it. Sorry, Mom!"

That Thanksgiving morning Jim had preached for twenty minutes in a blazing sun. Then he and Steve had given out Gospels and Viet kits to 500 soldiers. Major Duc (DOOK), a tough paratrooper and leader of over 53,000 people in that district, stood with his men and listened intently. This man was considered the best district chief in all Vietnam. He had been decorated by American Defense Secretary Robert McNamara for bravery and leadership. But this day was most likely the last time he heard about Christ.

On Christmas Eve, just two weeks before he was slated to become chief of the crucial Binh Duong province, two VC platoons mined his vehicle and riddled him with automatic fire, breaking their Christmas truce pronouncement. He was killed just one mile from our Quang Trung Induction Camp Chapel.

What a mockery! The province he served, Binh Duong, means *peace*.

14

Back Yard War

It was 1968, Year of the Monkey. Four-year-old Mona and toddler Tara were playing on the front porch of our home in Saigon. I couldn't believe that the raucous noise from millions of firecrackers welcoming in *Tet*, the Vietnamese lunar new year, had not disturbed the children's sleep. This morning, Steve, Kim Hoa, Mona and Tara were fine; it was their mom and dad who had headaches from lack of sleep.

Tet in Vietnam is like Christmas, New Year, birthdays and the fourth of July all bound into one. It is a time to look back to the past, to enjoy the present and to look forward to the future. But above all, it is a time to enjoy unhurried fellowship with loved ones and friends. For a few days at least, *Tet* was to be a delightful fragment of peace in this weary, war-torn land.

However, the tiredness Jim and I were experiencing was a cumulative thing left over from the hectic Christmas and pre-*Tet* season. We had participated in dozens of programs with Vietnamese military units. One especially exhausting day, a steady stream of Vietnamese officers had made their way to Jim's office with requests for Viet kits or anything which could be used as gifts for the men in their units.

"Jean," Jim confided to me later, "this whole affair could be made quite simple by handing over all the barrels of vitamins and crates of relief goods to the officers who make the requests. But that would not accomplish our purpose or bring any good for Christ's name. Our work would be just another give-away program, and that we do not want."

For these two missionaries our constant pleasure was in doing something helpful in the kingdom of God. Thus, at this special holiday season and in the face of possible danger, our team participated in the distribution of some 30,000 gift packets in distant places. At each site Jim and one of our Tin Lanh chaplains were given the opportunity to preach before making the presentation of the kits and the Word of God.

Transportation to a distant military installation or lonely firebase was never a problem. Upon request, a Huey chopper or a C-130 Hercules was made available for our use, complete with pilot and crew. Tons of supplies were loaded in the giant airships. The team even flew to the large Con Son (Cong SHONG) Prison Island. Separated from mainland Vietnam by a distance of ninety kilometers out into the South China Sea were 4,000 military and political prisoners incarcerated for terrorist acts, murder, rape, theft and repeated brawls. Unknown to us, this 1968 pre-*Tet* visit would establish a beachhead for our Lord Jesus. During four later visits to these notorious tiger-cage prison islands, a strong church made up entirely of prisoners would be established.

Zoom! Pow! Pow! Zoom! As the New Year celebrations continued, the lingering smell of firecrackers wafted into our bedroom.

"Mona, come here, please. It's time to cut your bangs," I called. There was no response. *Why do children hate to have their hair cut?* I wondered to myself.

Suddenly a chopper zoomed unusually low overhead. My heart skipped a beat. In one split second I understood that the repeated, loud explosions we had been hearing outside our bedroom window were not the pow-pow of fireworks at all, but the blasts of automatic gunfire not more than 100 yards away!

"Girls, into the house, both of you! Now!"

I burst into the study where Jim was working.

"Jim! That noise is not firecrackers. It's automatic fire! And it's down the street!"

"Let's go upstairs so we can see better!" Jim shouted.

Steve, who wanted to follow us, was told to stay inside the house and watch his sisters. We ran to the outside stairway of our building which led to the upstairs apartment of veteran missionaries Dick and Dorothy Taylor.

Two sleek Cobras, the Army's newest and most deadly helicopters, were swooping low over our house, releasing their rockets and raining a hail of fire on a target nearby. A huge column of black smoke arose from the direction of an electric power house as the rockets scored hits. With binoculars we watched American soldiers crouching on the porch of a house only seventy yards from ours, firing at VC somewhere below. Already bullets were whizzing past us and, from our position on the roof, we knew we were too exposed. We retreated to safer quarters.

Now what does a mother of four excited children do when a war is being fought in her neighborhood? Mop! I had planned to mop the floor, so mop I did. My heart was pounding, but I set out to do a very common task, one which the children had seen me do many times. I wanted to convey to them a message which even now is difficult to put on paper—like what not to do—like talk too much, like let your imagination run wild, like panic!

But the reality of our situation was beginning to clarify. We were literally witnessing a battle just 120 yards down the street from our house!

Tension mounted during the day. The air resounded with the crack of small arms including automatic AK47s. By now the communist troops were surrounded and desperate. American Armed Forces Radio broadcasted warnings every fifteen minutes. "All American civilians, remain in your billets. All major cities of South Vietnam are under siege!"

About 4 o'clock, a fire swept through the vicinity, burning several hundred homes a few blocks west of ours. Some VC were trapped, but many were hiding and using innocent civilians as human shields. One area near the Cong Hoa Hospital was hit and a row of prostitute houses commonly known as "100 Piaster Alley" was totally destroyed.

Our hearts ached. We watched scores of now homeless neighbors fleeing for their lives—a man with an old woman on his back; a mother with one hand balancing a bag hanging on her shoulder and the other tugging at a crying child; two Vietnamese soldiers supporting a limping comrade. They all came from the area just down the street from our house.

There was no letup of fire all day and, as evening approached, Jim laid out a plan. He took the family into the pantry-like room beside our kitchen where over a year ago we had dug a 5 x 2 x 6 foot-deep bunker. The Vietnamese and U.S. governments had strongly encouraged this plan when the U.S. military began bombing around Haipong and Hanoi. They figured the North Vietnamese might try to bomb Saigon.

The opening into the bunker was covered with an old wooden door. We never talked about that place—we just knew it was there if we ever needed it. Jim lifted the door and told me and the four children to climb down inside "just for practice." Over the past few months water had seeped through the dirt walls and had risen to about three inches deep. Several roaches and a dead lizard floated on top. The kids and I stepped down inside and Jim shut the lid. It was dank, dark and dismal inside that hole.

We practiced this routine a couple of times and then Jim addressed the children.

"If in the middle of the night Mom should wake you up and tell you to follow her, you must not say a word! Just obey. You will then climb down into this bunker. Do you understand? Remember, you must not talk. OK?"

That night a couple of neighbors worked out a strategy to guard the street on which we lived. Each man was supplied with a weapon by Americans also living on our block. The sight of this assault rifle both frightened and annoyed me for some reason. Yet both the American and Vietnamese forces had taken up strong positions on a street to the west of us and much of the firing was in the direction of our compound. What else could we do?

Our biggest fear was that the estimated eighty NVA communists who were surrounded at this time, would break out in small numbers and force their way into private homes. Certainly they would kill any Americans. The western portion of our yard was protected only by a small three-foot fence.

All night long C-130 planes circled our part of the city and kicked out bright orange flares which facilitated night vision.

Lead zinged and whizzed across our house off and on all night. Looking into the darkness and in the direction of the bamboo tree just twelve feet from our bedroom window, I could see the red tracer bullets making streaks through the leaves. Several bullets hit the bedroom shutter.

It was close to midnight when Jim insisted that I get some sleep. Both of us were exhausted since the night before we had been kept awake by the firecrackers. Finally I fell asleep, waking every few minutes to see if Jim was still on guard at the window. Thankfully the children slept soundly.

The next day the story was repeated, including the mopping scene. A heavy wooden window shutter was split open by a 30-caliber bullet that hit at head level a few feet from where Steve had been seated. Our house took at least nine hits—we had the slugs to prove it!

Since early morning, after the first big explosion at the power house, we had no electricity. The food in our refrigerator was thawing. I was forced to cook everything or else it would spoil.

Then—how positively bizarre—the stove ran out of gas!

Jim and Dick Taylor decided to venture out onto the streets in search of some place where they could purchase a tank of gas. Being *Tet* week, all stores had been closed before the fighting even began. The likelihood of finding gas was slim.

We had been told that the VC units had broken up into small groups, disguised themselves as civilians and were willing to kill for food. Therefore, before leaving, our husbands solemnly warned us under no condition to open the gate or allow anyone to enter. We agreed.

Jim and Dick had no sooner left when someone banged loudly on the metal gate downstairs. We peered over the wall from the vantage point of the upstairs porch and saw two uniformed soldiers.

"What should we do, Dottie?" I asked. "We promised not to open the gate. But how can we get them to leave?"

"I know," said Dottie. "Have you got any more of those toaster pastries from the World Vision warehouse? We will tell them that we have a special gift for them. Then we can just throw the pastry boxes over the gate. Maybe they will leave."

The plan seemed ludicrous, but it worked.

About an hour later, Jim and Dick returned with a tank of gas. Dottie and I related the story of our unexpected visitors.

"You did what?" Jim all but screamed. "Do you know what we just heard? All the holiday leaves for both ARVN and American military have been canceled. And there is a warning to have nothing to do with any Vietnamese soldiers who might be going about alone. The reason? Most probably they are fleeing VC disguised as ARVN soldiers! They kill and take the uniforms of the dead soldiers and then dress in them themselves. Good thing you did not let those two 'soldiers' in."

By the fifth day of the *Tet* offensive some 29,000 Vietnamese had been killed in cities all across the land. Finally, Jim felt safe enough to drive the children and me across Saigon to the Alliance Guest Home. He returned to guard our house and property, his fifth night on duty.

That night at the Guest Home the sound of automatic fire caused me to venture out onto the upstairs porch. On the street below we watched as four VC were apprehended and, with hands behind their backs, were cuffed and led away.

The next morning the children and I came down to breakfast to find a number of our missionary friends standing around in obvious distress. Some were weeping. Our field chairman had just phoned saying that six of our missionaries had been killed and one captured in a murderous night attack on the Banmethuot Mission compound. Ed and Ruth Thompson, Robert Ziemer, Ruth Wilting, Carolyn Gris-

Jim and Jean, Asbury College days, 1953.

Jim and Jean with Steve board the train for New York,
continuing by freighter to Vietnam, October, 1958.

Pastor Nguyen Linh baptizes a new believer from the Binh Son district. Pastor Linh and Jim teamed up for evangelism of Quang Ngai province's 900,000 Vietnamese.

Jim with Pastor Ngo Thai Binh. Pastor Binh saw hundreds, including a communist leader, follow Christ in the coastal fishing villages.

The "spy at my table." Mr. Vinh was the treasurer and fourth-ranking communist in Quang Ngai province.

In the village of Le Thuy the people received Jesus through evening *bo dao* evangelism. This fishing village was just six miles south of the Chu Lai U.S. Air Force Base.

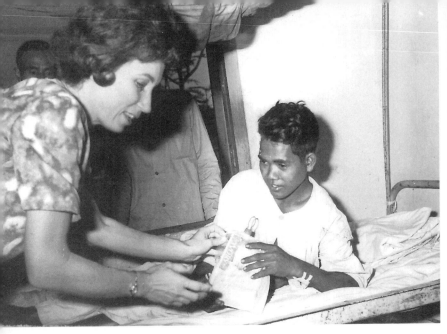

Jean comforts a wounded soldier and presents him with a Gospel of John.

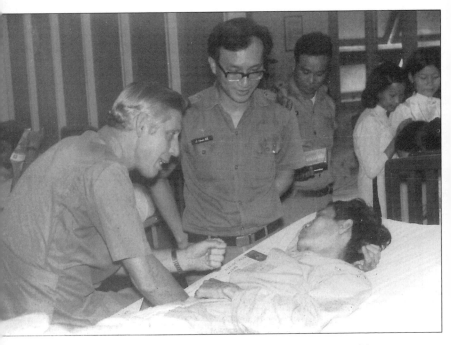

Jim leads Anh Trong, the boy-soldier with the amputated leg, to accept Christ at the Cong Hoa Military Hospital in Saigon.

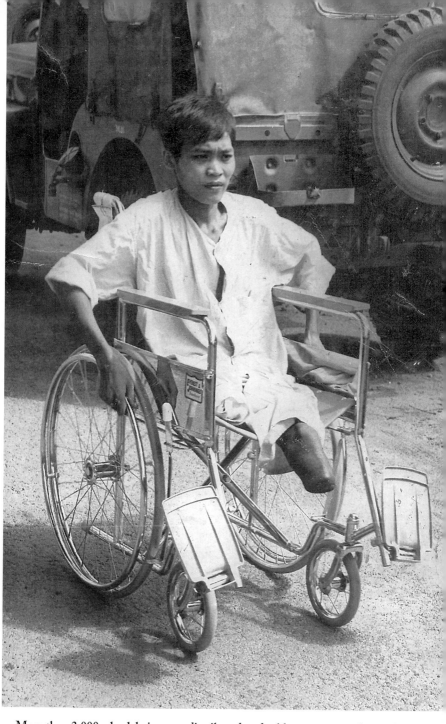

More than 3,000 wheelchairs were distributed to double amputees and paraplegics, all gifts from businesses and individual Christians in the U.S. and Canada.

Steve passes out Viet school kits to the children of a paratroop division.

Jim and Garth Hunt regularly visited Vietnamese troops on fire bases and outposts and always distributed Scripture portions.

Receptions were always enthusiastic during visits to lonely outposts, preaching and distributing Viet kits.

Gideon Bibles were received gladly by new recruits at the induction camp.

At weekly meetings at the Cong Hoa Hospital auditorium, several thousand wounded soldiers accepted Christ over a nine-year period.

A visit to Dalat School , Tana Rata, Malaysia, 1967.
L to R: Steve, Mona, Kim Hoa, baby Tara, Jim and Jean.

Every Saturday missionaries preached at the Quang Trung Induction Camp. Most of the 23,000 boys heard the gospel only once before being sent to the battlefields.

The roof of our sound truck, a gift from the Pocket Testament League, made an ideal platform for preaching to the elite Red Beret troops.

Tuesday evenings were spent at the Go Vap Military Prison. The men were guilty of various infractions against military law: drunkenness, brawling, theft, desertion, etc.

The PRC Mission house and compound lay in the path of the deadly Pinatubo eruption. Sand and ash measured five inches deep in the yard.

It took two days for these refugees, all new believers, to clear the lahar from the church property.

Our truck broke down almost every week for six years.
No wonder we called it "The Hypocrite."

Former nightclub crooner, Pastor Ador, and his wife Norma, became key partners
in the planting of three churches in the Death March Province of Bataan.

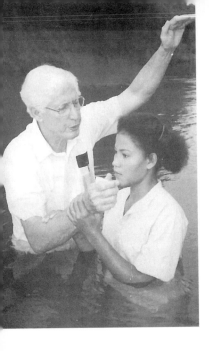

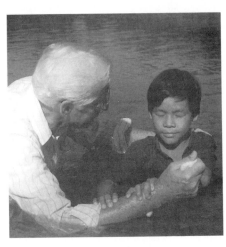

"O Happy Day" was the theme song on the fourth Sunday of each month when new believers testified to life in Christ and were baptized at the stream behind the camp. The Orderly Departure Program allowed hundreds of Amerasians, like some of these, to hear the gospel message.

The tall missionary Grandpa was the children's friend.

The refugee billets, measuring 9' x 18', provided a place
to love and laugh, encourage and comfort.

"Those who sow in tears will reap with songs of joy." Psalm 126:5

The Livingston family met in Penang in 1984. Unfortunately,
Mona and her family were absent due to canceled flights.

wold and her father Leon had paid the ulti-
mate sacrifice. Marie Ziemer was missing.

Alliance headquarters immediately ordered
all women missionaries and children to leave
Vietnam. Jim and I looked at one another in
disbelief. Because we had only a few months
left until furlough time, we felt at peace in re-
questing that we be allowed to return to the
States as a family rather than my taking the
children to Bangkok. Permission was granted,
and two weeks later we boarded a States-
bound jet.

Home never looked so good! What a contrast
were the quiet and peaceful evenings in St. Petersburg, Florida! The fragrance of orange blos-
soms floated through the window. During the
wee hours of the night, I heard the singing of a
Florida nightingale. Gone were the screams of
Phantom jets, the clackety-thud of choppers,
the drone of Hercules C-130s pushing flares in
the midnight sky and the sound of exploding
mortars in the distance.

At prayer time one evening I asked the children what they were most grateful for. Little
Mona replied, "That there is no more shooting."

Yes, we were safe at home. But Mona had
become an unexpected casualty of war. Several times each week for the next twelve
months she would wake up in the middle of the
night crying.

"Mommie, the VCs are coming. The VCs are

coming!" Mona would wail. One night she asked, "Mommie, are the VCs over in Tampa? Will they be coming to get us?" I always snuggled her close to my heart and did my best to comfort her.

During the day, Mona showed no signs of disturbance, but at night the dreams recurred over and over again. Mona had experienced war.

The *Tet* offensive was one year behind us when Rev. Willis Brooks invited me to visit Tenth Avenue Alliance Church in Vancouver, British Columbia to be the speaker for his second week of missionary convention.

In ten days I spoke twenty times. On Thursday evening the women of the church had a special program. After I had finished my presentation, Mrs. Brooks, a lady of very small stature, but a giant of a woman with a vibrant faith, pushed her little standing-box up behind the lectern where I had just finished speaking.

"Jean, before you are fifty women who know how to pray. Is there any personal request that you would like for us to remember in prayer?"

Immediately I thought of little Mona and her frequent nightmares.

"Oh, yes, Mrs. Brooks. I have a very personal request."

I told the women about Mona's nightmares of war, death and fears from the *Tet* offensive. The ladies promised to trust God and pray each day for Mona until she was delivered.

As I flew back to sunny Florida, I wondered how Mr. Mom had made out, cooking, washing and doing all the chores. I was sure this would be the last time Jim would volunteer like that again. And, of course, I wanted to tell him about my week in Vancouver.

That night I kissed the children and tucked them in bed. I had missed my mother jobs. I had missed hearing Steve tell about his seventh grade adventures. Kim Hoa always had a funny tale about school. Tara was a happy little toddler who loved flowers and animals.

And Mona. As I went to bed there was one big question mark in my heart. I prepared myself for the usual. But Mona slept peacefully all night! And the next night, and the next and the next! From the day I returned from Vancouver to this very hour, Mona never again experienced a nightmare about war.

We could ask a question here. Jim and I had prayed for twelve months regarding Mona's recurring nightmares. Why did the loving heavenly Father not answer our prayers? We do not know why. But we do know that in His sovereignty, God sometimes chooses to use others in answer to our need. Perhaps He wants us to be aware of the value and potential of corporate prayer, the united, fervent prayers of His Body. All we know is that God had heard the prayers of Mrs. Brooks and the "praying fifty." Our daughter was totally free from fear.

Today, Mona is a well-balanced mother of

three happy children, a gentle nurse and the wife of a fine pastor.

God can be trusted in times of war as well as times of peace.

15

Secret Place of Thunder

The Vietnam field chairman's annual report of June 1963 was an appeal for prayer and perhaps a word of prophecy. In 1971, God was indeed waiting in the wings ready to invigorate our souls and answer the request which had been voiced eight years before by Grady Mangham: "Above all, we need a spiritual revival that will sweep through the ranks of God's people here. Nothing short of this will make us adequate for the task before us."

Looking back on those years, I think it would be accurate to say that we missionaries were an earnest, energetic bunch caught up in the whirl of missionary activities, busy, busy, busy, always doing something for the Lord. Jim and Canadian missionaries Garth and Betty Hunt, led a team of ten nationals. During those war years we saw an unusual and abundant harvest of souls in the kingdom of God. Hardly a day passed that some Vietnamese youth, most of them soldiers, found forgiveness of sins in Christ Jesus.

In the morning our schedule might require a trip to the Alliance Press over in the big Chinese market sector of the city. That meant driving through incredibly congested traffic. Task completed, then, it might be on to the rehabilitation center where God had opened a ministry among war veterans who were feebly attempting to re-enter civilian life, only this time by means of stainless steel, plastic and leather straps and cumbersome prostheses.

Three mornings a week it was bedside visitation at the military hospital, followed by a brief rest at noon. In the afternoon there would be office work at the warehouse or a chopper trip to a distant military outpost near the Iron Triangle and the next day a 45-minute drive up the smooth, American-dollar-built Bien Hoa (BIENG Wa) Highway to the women's prison at Thu Duc (Too DOOK). While every day was different, they all had one thing in common—they were busy! Too busy!

Some of us third-term missionaries had been in the Vietnam war scene for ten or more years already, others even longer. We knew we were where God had called us. But the plain truth

was that the pressures of living in a country under siege were having their effect on many earnest and sincere missionaries.

Oh, we could have made a good case for ourselves and perhaps have raised a few questions to
try to justify our state of mind and soul. Were
there not three of our missionary staff missing,
having been abducted from our leprosarium at
Banmethuot in 1962? Had we not lost another
seven missionary colleagues during the 1968 *Tet*
offensive as the result of deliberate communist
barbarism? Had we not felt pain and sadness as
we watched our children being evacuated from
Vietnam and sent first to Bangkok and then to
distant Malaysia for their education? Had we not
traveled the city streets, where from time to time
grenades were thrown at random, where angry
university students or militant Buddhists demon-
strated violently and where insane terrorist acts
made the headlines in *The Saigon Bulletin* and
newspapers all over the world every day of the
week? Had we not witnessed the killing forces all
up and down the land and even in our own
neighborhoods? Did we not go to bed almost
every night and hear the rumble of distant B-52
bombing far out from our homes toward Tay
Ninh and the Cambodian border? The answers
were "yes, yes!"

May I ask still another question? What was
the measure of missionary success in this
blood-drenched land?

In many of Vietnam's forty provinces, from

the Seventeenth Parallel to the southern delta, our Alliance colleagues were seeing churches born by the power of the Holy Spirit. If seeing people pray to receive Christ is a measure of success, then of course we qualified. Souls were being saved by the hundreds in the hospitals, prisons and military camps. Furthermore, we had the attention of such renowned people as Bob Pierce, Larry Ward and Katherine Kuhlman to mention just a few, all of whom came to Saigon and visited our work. Corrie ten Boom was a special guest at our dinner table, as was Oral Roberts and his evangelistic team on another occasion. Billy Graham made special trips to visit the U.S. troops and invited all the Saigon missionaries to be his guests for dinner at the Rex Hotel in downtown Saigon. Jim and Garth had a special invitation to attend the Billy Graham press conference and our son Steve and Garth's son David tagged along just to shake hands with the famous evangelist.

Nevertheless, in the face of such attention, the grievousness of war had driven away much of our joy and, for many, mission work had become a frenzied chore. As one missionary so honestly stated, "I was as much disabled spiritually as many of our VN soldier boys were physically."

Jim and I were ashamed to confess that even in our apparent success, ministry had become old hat. We had given out and given out to others, but we had speculated too long on war, political demonstrations and security problems. The result was we were dry in spirit. One colleague overburdened with wartime weariness said it like this: "I have encountered the killing forces, not the North Vietnamese nor the Viet Cong, but my own emotional exhaustion and the corrosive fear that we are losing this nation." We had to agree.

It was in this disheartening set of circumstances that a very precious thing began to take place. A little band of three, Garth and Betty Hunt and I, began to meet in Garth's study at noon each day. Our purpose was to seek God's face in prayer for personal renewal and a fresh, new infilling of the Holy Spirit. In God's providence, the week before Garth had experienced a sports injury which caused him to be laid up at home with a heavy leg cast. Now there was time for quietness.

A week passed and already we had begun to feel refreshed in spirit. Jim joined our little group the second week.

"Since I can't drive now and have to stay here at the house in this cast," Garth announced one day, "I am going to use my time not only to pray but to do a little research as well."

All of us benefited from Garth's plan as he set out to read excerpts from the biographies and writings of men such as John Wesley, Andrew Murray, Charles Finney, George Whitfield and A.B. Simpson with but one question in mind: "What was the secret for victorious living and the obvious supernatural anointing of the Holy Spirit in the lives of these patriarchs?"

From Garth's digging into their writings and biographies, two things emerged. First, each of these men of God were used in the work of the kingdom in a mighty way; and second, each of these men had experienced a special time of seeking and waiting upon the Lord. The Lord confirmed to our hearts that we were headed in the right direction.

We pressed on in prayer each day from noon until about 2:45, the hottest part of the day when the body craves a siesta. Nonetheless, our daily work schedules and ministries never ceased and amid our various responsibilities either at home or on the road, God gave us peace of heart to meditate, to pray, to learn from His Word—and to wait.

Strange are the ways of the Lord! We thought maybe the Holy Spirit would come upon us like a mighty, tropical typhoon. Or His fresh infilling perhaps would be like an erupting volcano accompanied with supernatural power too awesome for words. But He did not come that way at all.

Yet He did come! In our prayer times, He came gently with silent footfall, wooing and melting, and we recognized Him in our midst as one recognizes the company of a true friend.

From the beginning of our time together, we lived with one absorbing passion—to know the blessed Holy Spirit in all the wonder of His Person so as to better make Christ known to the Vietnamese. At times a spirit of brokenness prevailed as the Spirit in prayer revealed the dark corners of our lives. He showed us that in the past when we had said, "I love You, Lord," that perhaps what we really meant was that we loved ourselves—our ministry, our program or our reputation.

We wept during those times of prayer day after day, wept because of our weaknesses and wept because of our unbelief and our sins of pride. But those times were not morbid and gloomy. Always following that blessed time of brokenness would be quiet joy and sometimes gentle laughter. The love and unity in the Spirit which we were experiencing were "like precious oil running down on Aaron's beard, down upon the collar of his robes." During those days the only thing that mattered was to please Him, to focus our whole being on the Person of Jesus and away from what others thought of our ministry.

Still on our knees, we were led by the Spirit in intercession for our fellow missionaries. Beginning at the Seventeenth Parallel, we traveled southward and before the throne of heaven we lifted up every missionary by name as the Lord impressed us.

The annual Vietnam field conference was scheduled for June and for the first time in many years the venue was Saigon, not Dalat.

The Saigon-based missionaries would host missionary couples in our homes. The missionary family in Vietnam was a deeply unified, brother/sister band of missionaries. Although some of our dear ones were discouraged and wounded in spirit by the scenes of war and the numerous unrelieved tensions, the Vietnam field was in no way divided in purpose as a Mission. The unity, love and respect for one another was field-wide.

As field conference began it seemed to us that the same Spirit of seeking the Lord which we had known in our small group now prevailed in the Mission. On the first morning, one by one, missionaries were prompted by the Spirit to stand and lay bare the needs of their hearts.

One single missionary cried out, "Lord, I am so depressed and lonely. I am ready to quit and go home." But through the power of the Holy Spirit, that missionary testified to being willing to remain, even without a mate.

Another colleague said, "I am new on the field and am bound by a strong fear of praying and speaking in public. Precious Holy Spirit, help me."

A missionary with training in two languages cried to the Lord, "I go into this village and the demonic forces literally bind my lips. Lord, free me for service." That missionary, revived and empowered by the Holy Spirit, returned to that same village and the results were marvelous.

One third-term missionary confessed debilitating doubts about the book of Genesis, and the Holy Spirit brought revival to his soul and a new awareneess of the sharp edge of His power and His presence.

One of our Dutch Alliance missionares from Thailand, Rev. Teo van der Welle felt strangely compelled to fly to Saigon and was used by the Lord in counseling and prayer during those days.

When the conference was over, missionaries returned to their stations and to their various tasks buoyant in the Spirit and manifesting spiritual nerve. They could not help but speak of God's fresh touch on their lives.

At the Nhatrang Theological Seminary, in Orrel Steinkamp's class on the history of revivals in the Church, the Holy Spirit came upon the students with such conviction that they had no desire for food or sleep. The student body assembled in confession and prayer for many days. As the Christmas holidays arrived, these students fanned out across South Vietnam with radiant testimonies of how God had personally met them.

As for Vietnam and her future, we had seen signs of crumbling from within. The U.S. was tired of the conflict and was talking about pulling troops out. Unknown to most, the North Vietnamese had no intention of withdrawing and were secretly digging their underground tunnels and infiltrating down the Ho Chi Minh Trail by the thousands.

Then God gave Garth Hunt a special assignment. With a request for prayer, one day Garth announced, "I believe God's Word is eternal and pertinent for today. I am taking God's message to the top! I am going to the members of President Nguyen Van Thieu's cabinet." Garth's holy boldness had become a unique part of his character.

The missionary continued.

"I am sure I can get an appointment with a good number of these men because of our contacts with the Vietnamese Women's Auxiliary." Representatives from this volunteer charity organization often accompanied Jim and Garth to various military units and participated in the distribution of Viet kits. All of these women were wives of government officials or high-ranking officers in the Vietnamese army. And most important, many of them were friends of Madame Thieu, wife of the president of Vietnam.

Backed with our prayers and armed only with the Word of God, Garth Hunt began entering doors at the top echelons of the Vietnamese government. He sat with one official after another and to each distinguished individual he gave a copy of God's Word.

"This is *Tin Lanh*, Good News," he told them. "This is God's plan of salvation for Vietnam and for the Vietnamese people. These are God's requirements to avoid what seems like the inevitable North Vietnamese communist

takeover! Seek God's face now while there is
yet time!"

The generals, the colonels, the heads of
state and Madame Thieu all listened to
Garth's prophetic-style message, but most
often the answer came: "It is most regrettable
that at the present time the Vietnamese com-
manders are extremely busy with the war and
just do not have time to seek the face of the
Great God of heaven. Maybe later."

April 30, 1975 arrived—and it was too late.
Vietnam fell to communism. As the last chopper rose from the roof of the U.S. Embassy, Vietnam silently closed her doors to the outside
world.

For two years after the fall, we heard nothing
from the Church in Vietnam, and all we could
do was pray. Vietnam was being plowed and
harrowed by the sinister tool of communism,
but her soil was still fertile. God's Spirit
brought our people through extremely difficult
times with His peace in their hearts. With
every trial and peril, Christians looked beyond
their suffering and tightened their grip on God.
They proved their faith and lived their songs
and God granted to them what I call "splendid
stubbornness." Little wonder that a great turning to the Lord of people from every segment
of society reached levels described as "without
number."

"There is no way to count the converts," ex-
claimed Rev. Doan Van Mieng, former presi-

dent of the Tin Lanh Church of Vietnam, and a long-time friend.

It is true. No one could have imagined the extent to which the revival fire would spread. In some places, especially in the highlands with the Koho people in Dalat, the Jarai and Bahnar tribes in Pleiku and the Radays at Banmethuot, the movement of the Spirit was accompanied by many signs and wonders. The testimonies of the saints sounded like something out of the pages of the Book of Acts.

Although exact numbers are unknown, at the date of this writing, official goverment records list the Tin Lanh Church as having 500,000 members!

Yes, revival came. It was God-initiated and God-sustained. God planted the hunger in our hearts. God quickened faith by His Word. We wanted only what A.B. Simpson desired years before—an enduement for service. God filled us anew with His Spirit to be His servants in bringing about His sovereign will to the people in the Land of the Smaller Dragon. And *Tin Lanh* had become the secret place of thunder—a place where the voice of God was so real that it might as well have been thunder.

16

Portrait of a Refugee Camp

"Jean, I've been thinking. . . ." It was drizzling rain, one of those rare, almost cool evenings in Penang. The year was 1988. The melody of tree frogs accompanied by the repeated dripping of water falling on palm fronds stole through the upstairs windows. We had experienced six monsoon seasons already while on special assignment as chaplains and teachers at Dalat School, our school for missioinaries' children in Southeast Asia. Now the slow, contemplative way in which Jim spoke instinctively caused me to sense that perhaps something big was in the offing. Jim's eyes were fixed upon me, and his serious expression confirmed that I was right.

"Have you stopped to think that we have

only six or seven years left before we retire?"

Jim continued without waiting for me to reply.

"I know that we both have been feeling concern for the tens of thousands of Vietnamese in refugee camps. We have always felt a deep empathy for the poor, compassion toward strugglers and sufferers. My favorite Bible story has always been the Good Samaritan. And so . . ." I knew he was giving me time for his words to sink in, "I think that, if we are ever going to work with Vietnamese people again, it ought to be now!"

I knew it! When you live with a man for thirty-five years, you can just sense some things without a word being spoken.

"Jim, I love Dalat School," I replied. "I would be happy teaching here the rest of my life. Yet I too have wanted to return to Vietnamese work. But how? The possibility for spiritual ministries in the various refugee camps seems bleak. The Moslem government has mandated rigid regulations and do not even permit missionaries to visit in the camp here in Malaysia. The U.N.-appointed director of the camps near Bangkok, a confirmed agnostic, will not permit a missionary to preach in her territory. The Hong Kong refugee camps and Ga Lang camp in Indonesia already have pastors. We cannot go back to Vietnam. So, how are we going to work with Vietnamese again?"

Our conversation on that rainy night in

Penang was the starting place. We were told that two camps in the Philippines were open for ministry to Vietnamese refugees. We were encouraged to take the plunge and will forever bless the Lord because our Alliance leaders allowed us the flexibility to move in the direction our hearts told us to move. And so, two days after our arrival in Manila, we were already on the highway headed toward the Philippine Refugee Processing Center (PRPC) in the boonies of Bataan, the infamous Death March province.

The trip from Manila to Morong, Bataan was a hot, dusty, five-hour drive. We watched the scenery change from the jam-packed, traffic-clogged streets of Manila to the verdant rice lands of Pampanga. Lush fields unfolded before the blue-green of the distant mountains. Unknown to us, lying hidden in that same mountain range, was an old grandfather of a mountain called Pinatubo whose fury we would personally encounter all too soon.

After four hours of dodging ox carts, dogs, goats and that most fearsome monster of a vehicle with the reputation as being the most dangerous animal on the island of Luzon—the "Philippine Rabbit," a bus system notorious for its reckless drivers—there appeared along the way a small, inconspicuous sign which read, "You are entering Bataan province."

Bataan—the name conjured up long-forgotten memories of the cruelties of World War II. In

1942, on this soil, American and Filipinos stood together under the constant fire of the Imperial Japanese Army. Besieged on land, blockaded by the sea, cut off from all sources of help, courageous defenders experienced all that human endurance could bear. Ultimately, the white flag was hoisted and 76,000 sick and starving men surrendered.

But the Japanese conquerors had made provision to transport only 25,000 prisoners to the incarceration camp at Tarlac. The result was a forced march under blistering tropical skies, that unforgettable, grueling ordeal which became known as the Bataan Death March. Japanese soldiers showed no mercy to the weak and either shot or bayoneted any American or Filipino prisoners who faltered along the way. From 7,000 to 10,000 died on this road of ignominy.

As we moved along we saw historic markers that showed silhouettes of figures bent low as if falling. These signs read: "Death March—kilometer 65," or "Death March—kilometer 30," and finally, at Bagac: "Death March—kilometer 1." There were memorials to the gallant dead all along this highway, but there was no vibrant church for the living to be seen anywhere.

A few minutes later we ascended the crest of a small hill and there, stretched out before us was a long white beach. The South China Sea glowed like beaten silver. At the dumpy little village of Morong the last signpost pointed to the right: "Philippine Refugee Processing Center—6 kilometers." We were almost there.

Our hearts pounded with excitement as we stopped before the guard hut at the entrance to the camp. A serious-faced Filipino security officer peered inside the vehicle as if searching for something.

"NPA came in last night and three Filipino peasants were killed in front of the Morong market. Just take precautions," the guard said. Later we heard that the communist National People's Army (NPA) controlled the third range of mountains just four miles away and indeed at times came to town to collect taxes and to kill with impunity. Satisfied that no stowaway was on board, the guard signaled us into the camp.

Since 1975, shocking stories of what refugee camps were like in Asia had appeared in numerous periodicals. Therefore, the orderliness of PRPC was a pleasant surprise to us. This camp was spread out for two-and-a-half miles facing the South China Sea. With its paved roads, hospital, dental clinic, post office, family counseling center, deep wells of pure mountain water, fresh air and surrounding physical beauty, this place was indeed the "Hilton" of refugee camps.

PRPC had study schedules for all age levels and its own bus system which daily transported children, youth and adults (over 17,000 indi-

viduals) to classes which ranged from kinder-
garten to American homemaking. For five
hours each day, six days each week, refugees
studied English as a Second Language (ESL).
The six-month crash-course curriculum was
uniquely designed to help the refugee enter his
new life in the United States. But there was
one factor for which the United Nations High
Commission on Refugees had not made allowance—the spiritual element. What about the
spiritual needs of these refugees? What would
we try to accomplish in this camp?

An encouraging example of the spiritual re-
birth that we wanted to see is the story of old
Mr. Khoa (KWA), who, standing as tall as possible, still measured only about four feet seven
inches tall and barely came to a little above
Jim's belt. He had been a nurse practitioner in
Saigon for several decades. Now half blind and
wearing spectacles which looked like they had
been made from the bottom of coke bottles, he
arrived straight from Vietnam. The unfulfilled
promises of communism and Mr. Khoa's disappointment with his former religious beliefs,
plus excruciating loneliness so common to elderly people far from home, had caused serious
depression. To Mr. Khoa, suicide seemed to be
the only way to peace of soul.

One evening while wandering about the
camp, Mr. Khoa found himself outside the
window of our Tin Lanh chapel. Never before
had he heard an American speak Vietnamese.

The message seemed "delicious" to his ears. The next night he found himself again beside the church window. On the third night someone invited the old man to come inside. When an invitation was given to accept Jesus Christ, Mr. Khoa was eager and ready to pray the sinner's prayer.

The Lord immediately delivered him from his depression and his long-standing smoking and drinking habits. What was equally outstanding, almost overnight Mr. Khoa became a persistent and dynamic witness for Christ. He spent numerous hours in the billets witnessing to his neighbors about his newfound faith. Evenings would find him back at the chapel, bringing along several friends, even whole families, ready to pray and accept Christ.

To satisfy my curiosity, I finally asked, "Mr. Khoa, how many souls have you led to Jesus?"

"Nearly forty," was his prompt reply as he went on to explain his strategy.

"Everything you teach in the New Believers Class, I absorb and then the next day I go out and give it to my neighbors! The thing is this . . . ," and Mr. Khoa lowered his voice as if he had a highly confidential bit of information to share with me alone. "I know the mentality of the Buddhist and the ancestor worshiper. Therefore, I can personally refute their errors and share with them the truth in Jesus Christ."

This, in a nutshell, was the unique way the Holy Spirit moved in our refugee camp. One excited and satisfied new believer told a friend to come to the chapel and hear the gospel for himself. Like old Mr. Khoa, hundreds of Vietnamese were dissatisfied with their former religious beliefs, ancestor worship, spiritualistic and animistic practices and Buddhism. All these practices were viewed by thousands of Vietnamese as impotent, dead systems. They were a part of the past which held little hope or validity for today.

Before we moved into the camp, for thirteen months we shared a small three-room apartment in the nearby town of Morong with a family of beady-eyed pack rats whose goal in life was to steal all sorts of our private possessions and then aggravate me to death because I could not catch the varmints. I attacked them with my hot glue gun, sealing up their holes in the walls with the ends of tin cans. But in the middle of the night I could hear them boring through the wall and in the morning there was evidence that they were back again.

Lovely blue rat poison did not tempt them, nor would they walk into a trap. It was a hopeless battle which ended in a compromise. I would let the pack rats live with us if they promised to give back all the things they had stolen before we moved. And it happened that way. I found their collection of pens, belts, papers and underwear under the dresser on the day we left the apartment and moved into the refugee camp!

Together with a Baptist missionary, we began an intense and exciting program of evangelism, counseling, teaching and pastoring the three Vietnamese congregations. The atmosphere in the camp was favorable for evangelism because in the evenings folks had free time to stroll around, play cards or sit and talk.

Therefore, on Saturday evenings our chapels were usually filled with the curious as well as honest inquirers who were ready to listen to a program of special music and a message from God's Word. Any given week anywhere from five to twenty-five people answered the invitation to receive Christ as Savior. This seemed to us most natural, for the Vietnamese have always believed in a High God of the heavens. Thus God became real to them when the gospel was accompanied with love and concern for their personal burdens.

One of our boat people with a gift of compassion was the lovely, moon-faced Co Hoa. Three times she and her ten-year-old daughter tried to break free and leave the tyranny of communism. Each time she was captured and hustled off to prison.

"We lost everything we owned to the greedy communists," Co Hoa explained. "Our house, our property."

Then followed a final and successful sea escape. She paid the price—a designated amount of gold in the form of rings and chains. (Gold was the chief medium of exchange for refugees fleeing Vietnam.) On her finger was her wedding band and, on the other hand, she wore a second gold ring mounted with a piece of green jade. This would be her bargain money should the inevitable happen. And it did!

Several days out of Vietnam and drifting on the high seas, the frail boat was attacked by Thai pirates. They stole everything of value: gold, food, kerosene. Suddenly, one of the pirates noticing Co Hoa's daughter, grabbed the pretty child and would have flung her to the deck had not Mother Hoa screamed frantically in protest.

"No! No! She not yet a woman! Leave her alone!"

Hoa pulled off her jade ring and thrust it into the hand of the grinning, lust-filled pirate. It was truly a miracle that neither she nor her daughter were molested.

Under the North Vietnamese political leadership, the people of South Vietnam experienced firsthand an appalling system that was wholly godless and completely totalitarian. For this reason, a majority of the refugees who entered the PRPC camp had cast aside many age-old customs with accompanying loss of moral values. On the other hand, we witnessed amazing spiritual hunger. The Lord used this unusual scenario to bring fresh hope into the lives of these people.

The supreme joy of our time at PRPC was

teaching basic Christian doctrine to hundreds of new believers. No one could be baptized until they had successfully completed over twenty-two hours of study in the New Believers' Class. Whether it was dry season or monsoon time, electricity or no electricity, these classes continued as we prepared them for baptism and a life of commitment to Jesus Christ.

We even required each person to take a written exam before they could be accepted as a candidate for baptism. And every believer could earn a beautiful copy of God's Word in his or her own language by memorizing and reciting ten passages of Scripture.

Whether in an ESL class or a weeknight activity at the church, the rhythm of the camp was upbeat. Soon these people, the fortunate ones, were going to the great "heaven-on-earth"—America. We, of course, told our Christians that their expectations were largely unfounded, that America was really not heaven-on-earth. But in their minds, and compared to communist Vietnam, it was. And so we prepared them to enter Vietnamese churches which were now functioning in over 100 locations in the United States.

Another interesting development occurred within our camp. Initially, all refugees were "boat people." But, because of the high mortality rate on the high seas due to typhoons and starvation, plus the vulnerability of these small boats to roaming Thai pirates, the U.N. High Commission for Refugees (UNHCR) devised an alternative plan. People who could prove that they had been "persecuted or had a well-founded fear of future persecution" by the communists were classified as political refugees and came under a new designation: Orderly Departure Program. There was no need to flee by boats any longer. UNHCR bought tickets for the entire family and they were on their way to our Philippine refugee camp by jet.

Then another segment of the Vietnamese population was given special attention by being included under the Orderly Departure Plan—the Amerasians. The Amerasian Homecoming Act played a significant part in the migration of refugees from Vietnam. In this act, the U.S. government agreed to accept Amerasians and their immediate families and to give them legal refugee status. Then the skeletons started coming out of the bamboo closets.

I remember my surprise when first seeing the Amerasians. I could not help but stare. Hundreds were black with kinky hair; others were light-skinned with brown or red hair. As the word Amerasian implies, these were children who were fathered and abandoned by American soldiers and certain American civilian employees during the war. They looked like Americans, but they spoke Vietnamese and acted like Vietnamese and, in their heart of hearts, were Vietnamese. How many Amerasians were there? The answer—67,000!

"I tried to disguise my daughter," said the former sweetheart of a guy called Bill. She handed me a yellow, aged photo of her GI boyfriend. "I shaved her head when she was a baby. Then I dyed her brown hair black hoping she would go undetected. But it was no use. She looks too much like her daddy!"

In Vietnam these Amerasian youth were despised and called *con lai*—"half-breeds, the scum of the earth." They were harassed, ostracized, sometimes made to feel so uncomfortable that they did not go to school, hence the high illiteracy rate, especially among the Afro-Amerasians.

Some were bought to work as servants for the more prosperous Vietnamese. And in dozens of cities there were the notorious "street kids," known for their cunning ways of survival. These Amerasian children were one of the unwanted legacies from the war in Vietnam.

Jim and I visited a family in Neighborhood #4 one morning. They had adopted an abandoned Amerasian girl when she was only three weeks old. The girl, now eighteen, saw me and she began to grin and giggle.

I felt uncomfortable until her mother explained this embarrassing situation.

"Oh, you are the first American woman she has seen in her life. She thinks she looks like you and this strikes her funny!"

"Well, O-O-O-O-O K-K-K-K-K," I said.

A dark-skinned young man called Minh was typical. I surmised that his father may have been Hispanic.

"Most likely I shall never know my real father," he said. "But I wish I could see him, just once! Oh well, things are OK now. For the first time in my life, I have found real love right here in this camp. I have a heavenly Father who will never leave me!" We missionaries from Vietnam thought the wounds of war were great, but the wounds of rejection and abandonment were equally destructive.

After a long, dark period of living under years of communist totalitarianism, the Vietnamese were probably one of the hungriest and ripest peoples in all the world to receive a knowledge of our Lord Jesus Christ. And so they came.

"Grandmother Pastor" was a term of respect which I felt I had finally grown into, but the Vietnamese had been calling me this since I was twenty-eight! "Grandmother, why is it that everyone hated us in Vietnam, but now at PRPC everyone likes us?"

"It's love, Quang. It's Christ's love!" Love in the Body of Christ drew hundreds of these unwanted young people to our chapels. And they found their Father.

"The LORD is a refuge for the oppressed, a stronghold in times of trouble" (Psalm 9:9). He is indeed a place of refuge for hurting refugees. During the fourteen years of PRPC existence, 7,443 refugees, including Chinese, Cambo-

dian, Laotian and Vietnamese, found refuge in
the safe haven of Jesus' cross. To God be the
glory!

17

Coconut Village

L eRoy Josephsen was always Jim's idea of the ideal missionary. LeRoy had helped open some doors into the PRPC camp by being the first evangelical pastor to minister there in 1980. Now he had another highly successful ministry—church planting among Metro Manila's population of 10 million.

As he drove us to the camp for our first visit, LeRoy said, "Jim and Jean, the best thing you can do for Bataan is to plant a church here. I mean besides the refugee work—plant a Filipino church along Death March Road. These people along the western half of the peninsula are desperately in need of a gospel witness."

LeRoy's words echoed in our hearts as we drove across the winding mountain roads of Bataan province. Our Lord Jesus said that we were to be His witnesses in Jerusalem, in Judea and Samaria. If the Vietnamese at the refugee camp were symbolic of our "Jerusalem," then where was our "Samaria"? It had to be the Philippine villages near PRPC. They too needed Christ.

The Philippine government had high hopes for Bataan after World War II, but business firms and foreign traders did not choose to locate in this historic province. It was too far from Manila, too inaccessible. Thus, most of Bataan's rural populace seemed doomed to continued high unemployment and poverty.

Driving through these villages we could see old snaggled-toothed men and proud young bucks loafing in the shade and massaging the thighs of their fighting cocks. Unemployed and bored, they waited for someone with 10 pesos to place a bet. I remember the words of one Filipino who spelled it out most emphatically, "Oh that my husband loved me as much as he does his prize rooster!"

The women living on Death March Highway still went to the stream each day with the family laundry. With pounding stick in hand, they beat the clothes on a flat rock near the edge of the stream. Everywhere there were young women carrying babies on their hips or in their wombs and a toddler or two following close behind. The poverty resulting from unchecked and out-of-control population growth was the one thing that grated on Jim.

Even more discouraging was the staggering

fact that one could see no Protestant churches along Death March Road! What LeRoy said was true. It seemed that the good news of the Lord Jesus Christ had yet to be brought to Bataan.

The refugee camp, however, was the one bright spot in Bataan's current history. PRPC had been an economic boost to nearby communities and provided employment for dozens of motorized tricycle drivers and domestic workers. The nearby villages of Sabang, Morong and Nagbalayong were profiting indirectly from the refugee camp by renting houses to ESL teacher supervisors and the members of various volunteer agencies working in the camp. From primary schools to market vendors, for one reason or another, everyone was glad PRPC was located in Bataan.

Thus while Jim and I waited for our house to be built inside the camp, we felt the Lord leading us to reach out to nearby Sabang. This strategically situated village was located at the entrance to Subic Bay and just nine miles west of Subic Bay Naval Base. Our goal was to plant a church in this village.

And so, with a Christian Filipino couple, plus an old World War II army veteran who had once been jailed for shooting an American in the foot, we set out to survey Sabang. I soon learned that the word "survey" has an entirely different connotation to a Filipino. We surveyed Sabang simply by walking slowly from one end of the village to the other smiling and chatting quite nonchalantly.

"The people need to get a good look at us!" our friends declared. And stare they did! We recalled how easy it had been to strike up a conversation with the rice farmers in Vietnam, but in Sabang we were greeted with only blank stares and disinterest.

"Next week we will return and preach," we told a few of the villagers. But no one smiled.

The following Friday afternoon we located a vacant lot surrounded by several *nepa* huts. We would be plainly visible from the road. Jim hung the loud speaker on the branch of a young guava tree and I began playing gospel songs on my accordion. Wide-eyed, dirty-faced children heard the music and came running, kicking up billows of choking dust. But the grown-ups seemed reluctant. One of our team members went out to the road again to invite passers-by to stop and listen. But no one seemed curious at all.

With the exception of the twenty or so noisy children who drifted back and forth, one hunched-back old lady and another woman of questionable reputation, our first outdoor gathering at Sabang could have been labeled a flop!

"Oh well, praise the Lord anyway! It's a start. Perhaps next week there will be more," I said.

Reluctantly, after nine months of Friday afternoon outreach at Sabang, we finally had to admit that we were getting nowhere. We had prayed, fasted and felt certain that to target this important village was God's will. But in all our years of mission experience we had never confronted such hardness and apathy. We had failed to establish a beachhead on the sands of Sabang.

Sensing that we were engaged in a spiritual conflict with unseen demonic forces as real as the coconut trees that crowded the village, we wrote to our home churches in the States and urged God's people to fervently intercede for lost souls at Sabang.

One day shortly thereafter, a young man appeared at our door.

"Pastor Livingston?" smiled the man. "God sent me to help you reach the people of Sabang."

Andy Castro was an enthusiastic Bible school student in his mid-twenties. From the start we sensed that here was a Spirit-filled young man. Within two weeks Andy had a collection of Sabang's children whom he taught to clap and sing to the Lord. When summer drew near, a Vacation Bible School was held in the shade of the coconut trees. The hardened hearts of the people of Sabang were beginning to thaw. Everyone was especially happy when we learned that Pastor Andy had fallen in love with a young lady from Morong. It seemed to us that the Lord was indeed smiling down upon a future Alliance church someday in Sabang.

One day Pastor Andy told us he was returning to his hometown to announce to his family his intentions of marriage and to make plans for the wedding. He asked if Jim would perform the marriage ceremony in December.

We gave Andy a small love gift and sent him on his way. But we were not prepared for the shocking telegram which followed four days later. Shortly after arriving home, Andy had suffered a severe asthma attack and died. Jim went into our bedroom and wept.

This devastating news triggered a series of events which once again we could not have foreseen. For three weeks Jim had been suffering from a tenacious flu virus and cough. Three hours after receiving news of Pastor Andy's sudden death, while eating lunch in the home of fellow workers in the camp, Jim fell forward onto his dinner plate unconscious.

Assuming that he had choked on a piece of food, I cried, "Lord, I plead the blood of Jesus Christ! Save my husband!" I jumped up, bent over his body and tried to pry open his mouth. But it did not appear that an obstruction in his throat had been the cause of the sudden attack.

Jim was lowered to the floor, his face a dark purple. He was still not breathing. After what seemed like an eternity, someone spoke. "Look! He's breathing!"

We immediately took him to the camp hospital for observation. The camp doctors recommended more extensive tests in Manila. Our Vietnamese and Filipino Christians, however, did not hesitate to take the more direct route to the office of the Great Physician by way of the avenue of prayer. They prayed for him day and night.

It would be two weeks before our schedule would permit us to go to Manila for tests at the Makati Medical Center.

The diagnosis? A Stokes-Adams attack with the uncertain possibility of it happening again. Thus we were advised to secure an emergency medical leave from the Mission and proceed to the U.S. at once. Fully expecting the stateside examination to prove that Jim needed bypass surgery, and being the avid reader that he is, he packed one large bag of his favorite books to enjoy during the time of recuperation. At least the long days of bed rest would be utilized by studying the Word of God and reading good biographies, Jim's lifelong passion.

The next week we flew from Manila to Florida. The night before the scheduled appointment at the hospital, Jim and I attended the Rainbow Springs Village Alliance Church in Dunellon, Florida. At the close of the evening service an invitation was given for any who were ill to come to the altar where the elders were waiting to anoint with oil and pray. Jim went forward.

Early the next morning, while driving to Ocala where the heart catheterization would take place, Jim and I felt no apprehension whatsoever. We had done exactly as the Word of God taught, and our family in Christ Jesus—the Vietnamese, Filipinos and Americans—were praying. Following the catheterization, the doctor would give us his findings. Thus I waited for the inevitable—bypass surgery.

"Well, Mrs. Livingston," the surgeon began. "I am pleased to inform you that I find no blockage whatsoever in your husband's arteries."

A sudden burst of joy surged from my soul as the doctor continued.

"Frankly, I found this hard to believe, so I went back and looked at the pictures a second time. It is true! I hope that my heart is in as good condition as your husband's heart when I reach sixty!"

Praise the Lord!

We stayed in the States another two weeks and visited the Vietnamese churches in Houston, St. Petersburg and Orlando. In each place we found our refugee converts from PRPC in attendance.

But our burden now was dual. Yes, the Vietnamese were our first love, but the plight of the poor in Bataan province was like a heavy weight on our chest, a heart problem which only the Lord Himself could fix. The evil one had frustrated our every attempt to plant a church in Sabang. We seemed no nearer to bringing the kingdom of God to Bataan than we were a year ago. The spirits which bound that province seemed to have won. Now what?

18

"Never Mind, We Just Pray!"

I t started over a pot of Swedish meatballs. The Christian and Missionary Alliance was nonexistent in Bataan province in 1989 when we first began working at the refugee camp. However, north of us in Zambalas province, there were four small Alliance churches. Hearing that a Zambalas district pastors' fellowship was to be held in Olongapo, we decided to just pop in and meet our Filipino church planters there.

Olongapo . . . Subic Bay . . . Navy Base . . . one of the world's most splendid natural harbors—all this and more. But to pleasure-hungry sailors it had become known simply as "Sin City."

Upon our arrival, we located the recreation compound not too far from the Alliance Bible

Church and found what we were looking for—a small group of pastors and their wives sitting under the shade of a *nepa* hut. We introduced ourselves. The Filipinos smiled and commented that without a doubt we had been sent by the Lord Himself. Then they insisted that both of us should share a message with them.

I do not know if it was Jim's white hair, our old memorized messages still fresh and upfront in our minds from our last stateside missionary tour or the Swedish meatballs, but the Lord gave us delightful and immediate rapport with our Filipino brothers and sisters. When it was time to say *adios,* there was not a meatball left in the pot and the feeling was unanimous—we would meet again next month.

Such was the beginning of an intense and satisfying working relationship with bold Filipino church planters. Jim shared his burden for the unreached Bataan province with its many thousands of poor peasants lost without Christ. He told the story of our struggles getting started at Sabang and about the sudden death of Pastor Andy.

"I feel a great burden for these towns and villages of Bataan, but I will be able to give only about twenty percent of my time to such efforts. I believe it is only by prayer that we will see anything accomplished for Christ in Bataan. If you brothers are willing, let us begin having one night of prayer each month. We will encourage each other and pray for one another's burdens."

And thus monthly nights of prayer were begun. Joyful in their singing, fervent in intercession, sometimes laughing, sometimes weeping, the Filipinos called out to the Lord with great expectation, believing that God Himself would step in and act on their behalf. And He usually did.

Another two months went by. We still felt the lingering sadness because of the sudden death of young Andy Castro. Then, a surprise announcement! During one of our nights of prayer, the head elder of the Olongapo church, Salvador Saturno, with a smile and a twinkle in his eyes, stated that God had just called him to Sabang!

Amens resounded loud and clear through the group. But Jim and I just sat there. Was this the breakthrough for which we had been waiting? Where would the funds come from to support this fine man if indeed he came as a church planter to Sabang?

I am the chancellor of the exchequer of our ministry. When it comes to money, I am a careful steward, more cautious than Jim. But I often lacked the almost carefree confidence in the Lord's supplying our financial needs that Jim naturally possessed. It was a serious question: Where would the money come from to support a church planter in Sabang?

From the start, we called our new church planter, with his penetrating enthusiasm and zealous heart for evangelism, Pastor Ador. He had known the Lord for twelve years already. He would join us in Sabang with full lay pastor credentials and the backing of CAMACOP, The Christian and Missionary Alliance of the Philippines. Ador also excelled in musical talent. In fact, Ador was a former nightclub singer before the Lord got hold of his life.

"Pastor, when you sing the babies stop their crying and crickets stop their cricketing," I often teased him. Ador had a gift of awareness regarding people's needs and with his training in Evangelism Explosion, he would be a valuable harvester in leading souls to Christ. But there was just one problem.

"My wife does not want to be a church planter's wife," confided Ador one day. "She is not excited at all about going to the strange village of Sabang, a place of only farmers and fishermen, no matter how beautiful the scenery! Norma likes city life." Then Ador added the phrase that in future years would be his trademark: "But never mind. We just pray!"

And pray was about all Jim and I could do. We had no funds to support this lay pastor and his family. We had no funds for renting a house or paying his utilities. We had no funds for Bibles or Christian literature, much less a guitar or motorbike. But what we did have was a zealous elder who believed fully in God's clear call in prayer as God's means to fruitfulness. And pray we did!

Things began to pop! We looked back over the nine months we had grappled with Satan's forces in Sabang and it seemed there were so few results. The powers of darkness at Sabang began to yield at the mighty Name of Jesus Christ, the Son of God. Pastor Ador led forty-three youth to Christ, twenty-eight adults confessed their desire to follow, and another forty-one children started coming to Bible classes. Faith and zeal are contagious. Soon Sister Norma caught the fever. Leaving Olongapo and her little sewing business, Norma became the children's favorite storyteller and a pastor's wife par excellence.

Although we did not know how the Lord would meet the needs at Sabang, He began to speak to friends in Pennsylvania, Texas, North Carolina and Alabama. Becky and Steve at Dalat school made the need known and their senior class sent help. A Christian businessman in Penang sent large gifts also. And each month when we returned to Manila for supplies, to make repairs on "Hypocrite" (our thirteen-year-old Datsun truck) and to receive our allowance, there would be Work Specials funds from faithful stewards in the States ready for ministry use. God was so good! A few months later, we purchased a lot on which to build The Alliance Church of Sabang!

The discipline of regular fasting and prayer, which for Jim and me had been a thirty-seven-year discipline, was becoming as common as going to Sunday school in Sabang under the leadership of Pastor Ador. The practice of this power-packed discipline was all the more fascinating since all these believers in Sabang were new in the Lord.

With a faith which says, "Never mind, just pray!" our lay pastor guided his congregation in a night of prayer once each month, as well as noon fasting and prayer time each Sunday. No wonder the powers of darkness began to tremble.

One of the members of Pastor Ador's congregation was handsome, warm-hearted Romeo.

"Before I knew Jesus, I could drink nine bottles of beer in one day," laughed the happiest Filipino Jim and I had ever known. Romeo was a man set free—delivered from liquor, from smoking, from gambling and from an intense macho mentality. "Christ came into my life, and now," Romeo pauses, shrugs his shoulders and laughs, "for me, only one girlfriend—my wife!"

Romeo worked for us part time as our yard man. At noon I would see him eating rice and reading God's Word with the enthusiasm of a child. When Romeo's first son was born, the happy parents named the baby Emmanuel, "because God is with us," said Romeo. Romeo became the first church treasurer of the Sabang Alliance Church.

The Spirit of the Lord was moving on the

shores of the South China Sea. Sometimes it was serving in His joy; at other times, as in the early days at Sabang, it was like hiking through mud. God's servants sowed the seeds of the gospel, sometimes with tears. But endurance brought joy, and our faith increased as we began to experience the rich harvest. In Vietnamese, the fifth verse of the twenty-third Psalm is translated, "My rice bowl is overflowing." That is how we felt about our Filipino ministries.

God must have been pleased also, because He enlarged our vision. "This can happen all along Death March Road. Other churches can be born!" I began writing to faithful praying friends. From this point on our motto would be: "Sabang, plus four more!"

19

In the Path of Deadly Pinatubo

T he news media wire services around the world crackled: "This is the century's largest volcanic eruption . . . Luzon, Philippines . . . Mt. Pinatubo has erupted after a 600-year sleep. Thousands are homeless."

Field conference 1991 was held at the mountain resort city of Baguio, Luzon just a week before the historic eruption. Paying little attention to news coverage, we had enjoyed the spiritual feasts, times of prayer, fun with fellow missionaries and last but not least breathing delightfully fresh mountain air. On the final day, as we drove southward toward Bataan, the sky became menacingly dark. Rain started about mid-morning and strong winds lashed "Hypocrite" till it shook.

"Probably the start of another typhoon," Jim remarked.

"I hope we can make it back to PRPC before the winds become so intense that electric power lines are downed and we get stranded."

Passing near Clark Air Force Base, we noticed a strange spectacle. Some of the townspeople were wearing white face masks! Turning off the super-highway near San Fernando, we pulled into the parking lot of a restaurant. We had no sooner ordered our food when the room was suddenly plunged into total blackness. Customers began talking all at once, but we could not understand Tagalog and did not know why they were so excited. Waiters found candles for each table. We hurriedly finished our noodle soup, paid our pesos and went outside. We still had over three hours more driving before we would reach Morong.

The storm continued. But something strange was hitting our windshield. It was muddy water! Jim squirted window-cleaning solution on the glass, but once again it was covered with more muddy rain. We turned on the headlights. Minutes later the muddy rain was followed by wet, muddy, sand-like ash.

Like the chicken in the children's story, I said, "Hey, the sky is falling, the sky is falling! Could it be volcanic fallout?"

It was only 1:30 p.m. but it seemed like midnight. The wet gray ash stuck to the headlights. The windshield wipers groaned laboriously and finally ceased to work. We had no choice but to pull over to the side of the road. Practically speaking, we were blind. Jim's side of the truck was being sandblasted by wind gusts up to eighty miles per hour. My side was not as bad.

"Roll down the window, Jean. Maybe you can stick your head out and see the road!"

I peered through the darkness. The Datsun's lights were not reaching out, making it impossible to see more than about fifteen feet ahead. What seemed even worse, wet sand was falling on my head and getting in my eyes. I pulled back inside the cab.

Then I got the bright idea that maybe by putting on Jim's cap and at the same time opening our umbrella outside my window, perhaps I could see the edge of the road and we could proceed. It worked. But Jim could not see at all. Our only recourse was for him to work the accelerator, the brake and clutch and I would steer the truck with my left arm while holding my head and the umbrella out the passenger side window with my right hand.

Down the road we went. There was no one alongside the highway and no cars on the road. From time to time I would holler, "Stop!" And retreating inside the cab once more, I cleaned the sand off my eyebrows, cap and umbrella. Then we would start out again.

Suddenly bolts of lightning zig-zagged in front of the truck followed by more lightning which flashed in a horizontal direction all about us. The lightning sizzled and popped, casting an eerie, orange light on the roadside. We grabbed glimpses of banana trees and co-conut palms bent low from the weight of the falling sand and ash. The sizzling sounds were that of electric currents in the air literally frying the falling sand and turning it into glass.

Hours later, we finally reached PRPC. It was 5:30 p.m. and still midnight blackness surrounded us. Wiping our headlights, we saw a scene not unlike that of a moonscape. Sand and ash, whipped by the typhoon, clung to everything. But not a refugee was in sight. They were huddled behind locked doors fearing the worst. Wild rumors, we found out, had circulated throughout the camp: "All Americans and Filipino camp authorities have fled to safety. And the peak of one large, nearby mountain is expected to explode soon. We are left all alone."

Of course, none of this was true.

We pulled up to our house and I went to the door. The house was locked. Where were the keys? The keys and the housekeepers were gone!

By 6 p.m. the winds had died and an uncanny, black silence engulfed the camp. Still the sand fell from the sky until it reached a depth of five inches on the ground. Now what to do? We were exhausted from the strain of the ten-hour trip. We simply had to get into our house.

Bang! Bang! Rifle fire? Hundreds of rifle shots! My first thought: "The communists certainly picked a fine night to attack the camp!" But when large limbs from nearby trees came crashing to the ground, we realized that the sounds were not rifle shots at all, but the crack of hundreds of limbs from mahogany, teak and mango trees snapping like toothpicks under the weight of tons of sand and ash. Most of the cracking sounds were coming from the rain forest across the river below the camp.

How much longer would the volcanic fallout continue? We had no way of knowing. We simply had to get into the house! But how? Our house, as do most houses in Asia, had iron burglar bars embedded in the window frames.

"I've got to find something to break these bars loose," said Jim heading toward the back yard. He found a stout iron bar we had used for digging holes. "Now, which window? The bathroom window is the smallest and would be the easiest to break into," reasoned Jim.

With the car lights beaming in our direction, Jim climbed up onto the washing machine located in a closet-like room outside the house and directly under the bathroom window. He rammed and pried the window with the iron piece for about twenty minutes before the security bars finally yielded, leaving a fair-sized opening.

"OK, Jean, climb up here now and all you have to do is go through the window, drop down into the shower stall, come around and open the front door. A piece of cake!"

It sounded easy. With both of us standing on the Maytag and with Jim's help lifting and pushing from behind, I got both feet over the window sill and started to ease down the inside bathroom wall. But my position was face up and the opening between the bars was narrow. Besides, I just don't bend that way!

"Stop!" I hollered. "Turn me over!" With Jim's help, I managed to get turned over, tummy side down this time, and as he pushed on my shoulders, I slowly began to go down. But there was a problem. As I descended, my jean skirt ascended! It came to an impasse in the region of my hips and I was stuck—a real live dangling participle!

Finally, a few minutes later, Jim and I were both inside the house and praising the Lord for bringing us home safely. Yet we could not help but wonder if there would even be a tomorrow morning.

About that moment, the house began to vibrate. The refrigerator began to sway back and forth and the teacups began to dance on their hooks. Earthquake!

I do not remember that we ate anything before giving up and going to bed that night of June 15, 1991. The house vibrated repeatedly throughout the night. Later we learned that over 350 volcanic tremors had rocked Bataan and other provinces. Geologists and scientists would later explain that the tremors were the result of billions of tons of lahar (water mixed with lava, sand and ash) being spewed as high as twenty-five miles into the sky.

At 5:30 a.m. Sunday, June 16, a dim light awakened us to a gray sand and ash-covered world. Mt. Pinatubo had dumped millions of tons of sand and ash on an area half the size of New Jersey. In places it was forty to sixty feet deep. A geologist predicted that for at least ten years of rainy seasons the lahar would wash down the mountainsides causing more devastation to crop lands, towns and villages.

From our bedroom window we peered outside. The dog was walking over the yard, her feet sinking down five inches making little holes in the top layer of the grey sand. Everything was totally covered. My plants had been buried alive. The bougainvillea were bent to the ground and painted gray. Even the fence was layered with the stuff.

But I was not prepared for what greeted my eyes when I walked from our bedroom into the living room. Everything was white! The cement floor, the silk flowers on the table, the couch— all covered with white ash! It seemed that the stuff had seeped in through the space between the glass louvered windows during the night. Now I understood the gritty feeling on our sheets. We too had been dusted with ash!

Jim's first task was to clear the roof. We did not know how much weight it could stand.

Three Vietnamese boys from the church were enlisted and they began shoveling the sand.

About 10 a.m. that first morning, a Filipina friend brought us a jug of water. We would not have electric power for another five days. Even at that, we were some of the fortunate ones.

That afternoon, our friend Tim, who with his wife had left the camp when the fallout began, returned. He had literally run the distance from the Base to PRPC. He told of the devastation of the jungle along the route and of the Filipino *nepa* huts which had collapsed and lay buried in the wet sand. We also discovered that 14,000 American servicemen and their families were in the process of being evacuated from Luzon. Over 100 buildings at the Subic Base had been destroyed, including one of the large chapels. Such was the destructive power of the heavy, wet lahar.

Ash was still falling when the gigantic clean-up began. The Filipinos called it "Operation Desert Sand." Someone issued face masks to workers because breathing the ash-laden air irritated the sinuses.

The birds left the area and there were no insect noises. The silence was broken only by the sound of five bulldozers working twenty-four hours a day pushing sand into huge piles to be picked up, hauled to the edge of the ridge and dumped. The herd of cows that freely roamed the camp did not have grass to eat, so they resorted to eating out of the garbage cans of the refugees. It would be two months before the camp was back to normal.

Each day the Lord comforted us with His Word. His presence was very real. He sent tokens of His care to encourage us. For example, even on that first morning, a courageous hibiscus flower dared to lift its head out of the sand and wave a flash of orange and red. Perhaps confused by the dull gray skies, the tiny 4-o'clock flowers under my kitchen window opened much earlier in the day, their fuchsia color and sweet fragrance an encouragement each time we passed.

Yes, June 15, 1991 was a day to remember. Bataan and neighboring provinces had experienced five natural phenomena: a volcanic eruption, a fierce typhoon, an eerie, orange, lightning storm, total eclipse of the sun for six hours before normal nightfall and protracted earthquakes and tremors. This tragic convergence of destructive physical calamities, all in one twelve-hour period, brought great suffering and left thousands of Filipinos homeless.

But we were kept! Unknown to us we had been driving fourteen miles from Mt. Pinatubo when the major eruption occurred. It was not a coincidence that our mighty God in His mercy ordained that at that very hour of eruption, a typhoon occurred. Had it not been for that typhoon which blew a major part of the ash out into the South China Sea, we could have been buried alive.

A total of 717 people dead, 50,000 houses destroyed, 70,000 houses partially damaged, 651,000 individuals jobless—these were the sad statistics reported in the *Manila Bulletin*, October 7, 1991.

Immediately the Council of Philippine Evangelical Churches led by Dr. Jun Vencer, an Alliance lawyer/pastor, began plans to reach out and bring practical help to these hurting thousands—another time of sowing seeds of kindness with tears.

But in spite of the eruption of Mt. Pinatubo and the extraordinary natural phenomena which accompanied it, God has not forsaken the Philippine Islands. He is continuing to build His Church.

20

A Violent Goodbye

Fear? If Jim had asked me if I were afraid, I would have immediately responded, *"Of course not!"* But hadn't the refugees themselves already implied that our house on the edge of the ridge was much too vulnerable?

The Philippine Refugee Processing Center, our home, our camp, our field of harvest for the past six and half years was in the final phase of closure. Only a few Filipino neighbors remained on the west side of our property and they were leaving camp. Our home had become isolated and unprotected.

"Tell me honestly, Pastor Ador," Jim began one day, "what are the risks in our living here now since our camp will be closed by the end of '94?"

"Pastor" answered our always cheerful church planter with a note of seriousness in his voice,

"You know, it is very easy for 'them' to come up from the valley. In fact, your back yard would be an easy place for 'them' to enter the camp. It is not as safe for you now as when the Vietnamese lived nearby.

We considered Pastor Ador's words, but our concern at this time was not the NPA (Filipino communists) who supposedly controlled the third range of mountains behind our house or the robbers in and around the camp who were determined to plunder every building of worth. Our main concern was the angry, dissident faction of Vietnamese who were even at that very hour staging a sit-down demonstration in the compound.

Who were those 442 Vietnamese protestors? Who were those who had been sitting in front of the UNHCR every day for three weeks now (some all night), their conical-shaped hats the only shade from the blistering sun?

We passed the now abandoned billets of Neighborhood #7. The doors on each billet were nailed shut. Gardens were overrun by weeds. Slim papaya trees pointed to the sky, but there was no fruit, for there was no one to water the ground now. Happy Vietnamese children no longer played Chinese jump rope on the shaded sidewalks. Grass had begun to grow over the soccer fields and a crow squawking from a bare tree branch was all that was left.

It was about one kilometer from our house to the abandoned World Relief Clinic building where we had been worshiping with the small remnant of believers still left in the camp. This building was in plain sight of the demonstrators who eyed us suspiciously each time we passed. Many of the men wore a white muslin strip or sackcloth tied around their foreheads, the age-old sign of death and mourning in Vietnam. Except on these funeral bands, in bold, black letters were printed angry words: No Repatriation! These dissident refugees were coming together to say to the world, "We would rather die than be sent back to Vietnam."

Two weeks before, ringleaders at the demonstration site had requested and oddly enough been given permission to use the camp's public address system. Several times each day they blared their protests against the Philippine government, the UNHCR and the new command which would force everyone to transfer to the refugee camp in Palawan Island. The move, as they feared, was the first step toward forced repatriation back to Vietnam.

Who were the 442? They were desperate individuals who had been pulled out of the Orderly Departure Program. There were valid reasons why these families were being denied admittance to the U.S. Many months prior to this time, during the initial screening process back in Vietnam, affluent Vietnamese had lied, falsified documents and bought Amerasian youth. They concocted stories of how "with a heart of mercy" they had "adopted" these unfortunate children sired by the American soldiers. Their so-called adoption and identification papers, even old photos of GI Joe with his arm around his Vietnamese girlfriend, were proof positive. The cleverly contrived fraud would be their free ticket out of Vietnam.

But the stress of overcrowded camp life exacted its toll. Most of the Amerasian youth living with these pseudo-families were little more than servants. They too were required to study and follow the rigid English program the same as the "parents." They too were required to do maintenance work two hours each day on the campgrounds. But back in their billet there was water to haul, stacks of laundry to wash by hand each day and meals to prepare. Plus there was heaped on top of it all the unending harassment of the "family."

A blow-up seemed inevitable. The Amerasian says to himself, "I am out of Vietnam now. I do not have to put up with this. The people I am living with are not really my family, and they did not raise me as an adopted child. They only bought me, paid my mother big piasters, like gold chains, bracelets, rings, all to get themselves out of Vietnam. Now they treat me like trash!"

Other young men, also to be returned to Vietnam, were the "monkey house boys" who had lived in and out of the camp jail for a number of years. Because of these crimes such as repeated brawling, rape, drugs, habitual breaking of the liquor ban and even murder, they too had been disqualified by the American immigration laws from going to America.

These were the 442, the dissident ones, who in desperation were willing to try anything to draw the attention of the world to their miserable plight. Everyone was grabbing at straws, thinking that perhaps the demonstrations and their pleas for what they believe was justice would attract the attention of a reporter from the *Manila Star* and eventually the world press, or even better, the Pope himself, who would be visiting Manila that month. Of course they never once mentioned the real reasons why they were not going to the United States—the lying, cheating and harsh treatment of their "bought" Amerasians. Some of our believers were in this "reject" catagory. Our teaching for them had been simple: The Bible is clear—we should obey civil authorities over us.

Then our Christians and we missionaries became their scapegoats. The resistance leaders in the camp incited some of the Amerasian young men who were little better than rawboned hoodlums to begin a series of beatings, stoning the roofs of our Christians' homes at night, stealing their chickens, ducks, clothing and even pots and pans.

We visited Brother Tu, a recent new believer who had volunteered to obey the U.N. and go to Palawan. We found his door locked although it was only 7:30 in the evening. Finally, the door opened slightly and someone peered out through the crack.

"Brother Tu, we knocked and knocked. We thought you were asleep!" said Jim.

"I heard you knocking, but I thought it might be *them*," was Brother Tu's answer. "Last night they stole my four ducks, took them right out of the pen and I did not even hear them. To-night I decided to lock up early."

Another friend, Bao, who in Vietnam had stubbornly refused to follow communism and lived as a fugitive for over fourteen years just a few steps ahead of his communist tormentors, came to our house and with a mixture of deep-est anxiety and bitterness said, "It was because of fear tactics that I left Vietnam! Now here in this place, they are threatening to beat me! Please let me stay here at your house for a while."

It did not surprise us that Jim and I, along with our Baptist co-worker, were vilified in the mouth-to-mouth propaganda which spread throughout the camp: "All the Tin Lanh people and their leaders (that meant us) are lackeys of the American government. . . . They work for the CIA and . . . force Christians to compli-ance with the U.N. government order." Smear tactics of this sort we had not experienced in all the war years in Vietnam!

The issue truly pressed home when we learned that some of the angry refugees were threatening the life of our friend, the Baptist missionary! *What about us?* we wondered.

Naturally, in these times of intense stress, Jim and I were drawn very close to the remaining seventy believers. It was true that most of them had done wrong in cheating to get a free trip to the States. They had been exposed, and now, realizing their mistakes, had repented and yielded their lives to the Lord Jesus Christ. They also were willing to be submissive to the government's authority over them and be transported to the Palawan camp knowing that they would eventually be deported to Vietnam. Attendance at the chapel on weekends remained strong and a group of about twelve continued to meet at 5:30 each morning for prayer.

The dilemma of the camp closure dragged on another two weeks until it was Christmastime. Our last celebration of the birth of the Savior in the refugee camp was a memorable one, joyful in spite of the threatening clouds which hung over the camp. With hearts of thanksgiving we ate our final fellowship meal together and took many photos of ourselves standing in front of the scrawny Christmas tree.

Finally, the day of departure from the camp arrived for the first group who had defied the threats of the angry and secretly volunteered to go to Palawan. Mrs. Chau met me after early morning prayers. With hushed voice she said, "We have just been notified. Tomorrow is the day. We will have only thirty minutes advance notice. Then we go. We are not supposed to tell any of the others!"

"OK," I said. "Come and tell us immediately after you are notified."

I could hardly sleep that night, fearing that something might go wrong or that perhaps one of our Christians would be hurt during a midnight raid.

About mid-morning the next day, Mrs. Chau's daughter arrived on her bike.

"Grandmother, now is the time!" she told us breathlessly.

We jumped into our truck and three minutes later were in front of Mrs. Chau's billet. We quickly transferred the Chau family's baggage and an odd assortment of precious junk to our truck. Filipino staff members were already evacuating a number of other refugee families by their vehicles as well.

Puzzled neighbors gaped at us in angry silence. We were assisting the first volunteers in leaving the camp in broad daylight right under the noses of the very ones who had threatened their lives.

In another couple of minutes, we were at the rendezvous place about a half mile outside the gate. Two big buses were parked in the middle of a rice paddy waiting for the excited refugees. From here they would be transported to the transit camp in Manila for one night and then on to Palawan.

The original Plan A had been to transport the

entire number by a Philippine navy ship. This way they would have been able to take all their possessions. But this strategy had failed because of the camp rebellion and lack of cooperation.

The camp authorities switched to Plan B which meant they were forced to use the commercial planes of Philippine Air Lines. And that meant strict observance of the baggage allotment—about thirty pounds per ticket.

Scales were set up under a big tree and the weighing-in process began. Things once thought important were now on the verge of being discarded because of "no room" or "too heavy." One of the officers jerked a doll from a young girl. The child cried loudly and everyone stared at the officer. He was forced to change his mind and return the doll.

Plastic junk, dog-eared magazines and old clothing lay strewn all over the ground. Even envelopes and letters, considered so precious by Vietnamese, were abandoned in the rice field, abandoned by those who had almost nothing. It was one of the saddest spectacles in all our years of missionary service.

After a two-hour delay, all baggage was weighed again and loaded in the buses. Everyone wanted a window seat so as to have one last glimpse of the majestic mountains and picturesque valley, and us, their friends, who stood waving until the bus reached the curve.

"Goodbye, PRPC. Goodbye, Bataan."

Back at the camp, an army of disgruntled dissidents continued to dig in their heels and scream their protests. There followed an article in the Manila newspaper which showed photos of refugees mounted high on the roofs of their billets. With plastic jugs in hand, they claimed they were going to pour kerosene onto their bodies and set a match to their clothes. They climaxed their protests with threats of mass suicide should they be forced to make the move to the Palawan camp. Fear became a way of life for many of us those last few weeks at PRPC.

On January 6, a blessed, heavenly peace, free from all fear and anxiety, came upon me. It was as real as a cool breeze off the South China Sea. It would be two months later before I understood what happened in the heavenlies during those days.

Lynne Hultquist, a math professor at Penn State University wrote: "In January I was awakened during the night with a heavy burden to pray for you. Did anything unusual happen at that time?"

"Yes, Lynne, God bathed our hearts with His peace. Something unusual did happen!"

The camp closed as scheduled. Twenty-six days later, with mixed emotions, we too said goodbye to this place we had grown to love. The entire camp compound and the keys to all the buildings were turned over to the Philippine government. Pastor Ador secured a lay pastor and his wife to occupy our home. The camp administrator, because of Jim's timely intervention, granted The Christian and Missionary Alliance of the Philippines possession not only of our Mission house, but the two camp chapels as well. Hallelujah! If the plan of the municipality for developing a ninety-hectare technology park comes to fruition, we have chapels and staff ready to meet the spiritual needs of the populous. God is so good!

And so, Jim and I left PRPC. Had all the slander and insults somehow caused us to love our Vietnamese people less? We answer very firmly, "Not at all!" We would have liked for our last months in the camp to have been as satisfying as the six and a half years that preceded them. But they were not.

Yet on our part we felt no cause for lingering anger. For us, despite what we might call a highly unpleasant, but manageable burden, our bonds of commitment to a hurting Vietnamese people remain as strong as ever.

21

More Joy Than Tears

E aster 1995 was our last Easter in Southeast Asia. We had become "long-stayers" at the Manila guest home and were making do from our one-room efficiency apartment. A crock pot, an electric wok, a small microwave and a laptop computer were our only tools for housekeeping. We were busy closing down twenty-eight years of service among the peoples of Southeast Asia, most of those years in the Land of the Smaller Dragon.

Sunday we would again worship with our Vietnamese brothers and sisters in Christ, but this time it would be at the transit camp. This was a temporary holding place for refugees built right beside the jet runway of the Manila International Airport. At the transit camp, everyone lived together, their only privacy being the thin plywood walls or flimsy curtains which separated one family cubicle from another. Along with all of us in Manila, the refugees shared the insects as well. In good humor, they commonly referred to this camp as "Mosquito Bite Hotel."

Psalm 126 had become a guiding light to Jim and me over the years as we served God among the peoples of four nations: the United States, Vietnam, Malaysia and the Philippines. We saw ourselves as part of "those who went forth" bearing precious seed and later reaping a glorious and joyful harvest. But now, here in Manila, we were a bit nostalgic.

Over the years God had placed in our hearts a sympathy with hurting people of all kinds. We had worked among the 343,000 Southeast Asian refugees who had passed through PRPC's gates. These were perhaps the hardest years of our missionary career. Yet strangely enough they were some of the most profoundly satisfying years. It had to be because of the Holy Spirit's uplifting power of joy which He gives to His sowers and the deepened sense of comradeship with our people, all of whom were sufferers.

To state that between 1989 and 1995 more than 7,400 refugees accepted Christ as Savior and were baptized at PRPC in no way adequately tells the story. Behind every face was a story of pain, sacrifice and of lives plunged into almost every imaginable emotional distress. Yet our camp became for hundreds a place where their bruised hearts began to experience some of heaven's healing balm.

I chuckle to myself. Have Jim and I become

two sentimental old-timers given to day-dreaming and the telling of old stories? We know we are soon to leave the Orient. A vast ocean will separate us from the yellow-skinned and brown-skinned people that we have come to love. Is it not understandable that we should take time to bless the Lord and remember?

The memory of our unexpected return to Vietnam in 1988 still leaves me excited. No one expected us. Little wonder my hairdresser whom I led to the Lord years earlier, upon seeing me enter her shop, gasped, "A ghost, a ghost!"

The trip to Vietnam was an anniversary gift from our four children. For us it was the chance of a lifetime to encourage certain saints and to assure them of our constant prayers over the years.

One of the key people we had hoped to visit was the former president of the Tin Lanh Church of Vietnam, Rev. Doan Van Mieng. Years under communist occupation had not clouded this man's gracious Oriental manner. But on this visit he wasted no time with the usual courtesy talk, choosing rather to launch directly into serious conversation.

"We have only a little time together," he said. "Please let me tell you as much as I can so that when you return to America you can share the good news with our brothers and sisters in Christ there."

Sensing our unvoiced questions, Rev. Mieng

approached the subject of religious freedom. His remarks were classic.

"Free?" asked the wise old man. "A fish in the ocean is free; a fish in a river is free and so is a fish in a bowl. We are free, like fish in a bowl."

We sat in silence eager to hear more.

"The Tin Lanh Church had 400 church buildings when Vietnam fell to communism in 1975," continued the man of God. "And even though a hundred buildings have been either confiscated or destroyed, the number of believers in Vietnam at the present time is so many that we cannot adequately number them. Especially is this true with the tribal people in Banmethuot, Dalat, Pleiku and Kontum. There is no way to count how many have received Christ in recent years."

Rev. Mieng watched our faces, giving us time to praise the Lord.

"I have been told," continued Rev. Mieng, "that the tribal Christians are saying that they no longer need church buildings. The Lord gives converts even in the jungle!

"Here in Saigon, however," he continued, "the number of times when we can meet together at church is limited. But we find other ways to carry out the Lord's work.

"When there is an engagement party, a wedding, a funeral or even a birthday celebration of a newborn infant, all of us pastors go to commemorate the event. They do not know that we use that time to do the Lord's business

and we always preach the gospel to the unsaved guests. Many believe at these times of
celebration."

The Holy Spirit, we found out during our visit,
had inspired His servants to spread the gospel in
many unique ways. In one rural village, everyone
works six days a week and on Sunday they rest.
But Sunday is the day the communist maintenance supervisor chooses to attend to the more
obnoxious jobs in the neighborhood.

"Are there any volunteers?" barks the supervisor. No one speaks, for these Sunday jobs always include cleaning the putrid, public
latrines. Finally, certain "unlucky" ones are appointed for the nasty chore.

Once a year another unpleasant job is scheduled on the Sunday "day off"—that of cleaning
the village well. Again, the officer asks for volunteers. The Tin Lanh pastor steps forward.

"I am willing," the pastor states casually.

He collects his brush and bucket and allows
himself to be lowered into the dark, slippery
well by his "helpers." There he begins to scrub
down the cement walls of the well. After a few
minutes, a carefully conceived plan begins to
unfold. Someone feels sorry for the pastor and
requests permission to descend into the bottom of the well to help with the cleaning job.

Mid-morning, the supervisor drifts off for a
cup of tea and our pastor seizes the opportunity he has been waiting for—the real reason
he volunteered to clean the well. Another

"helper" is lowered down into the well. A couple of minutes later that one emerges again only to be followed by yet another "helper," and still another and another!

What is happening? The pastor is baptizing his new believers in the bottom of the well! And it is all done right before the noses of the godless communists! Hallelujah for Jesus!

A certain Saigon pastor is inspired with a plan and requests permission to take his friends swimming at a beach town. But the two hours it takes to drive to the beach are carefully utilized by the pastor. He uses the time to teach a basic Christian doctrine class while chugging down the highway. The interior of a rickety old bus becomes a classroom where there is no threat or interruption from a communist police officer.

An earnest young layman with Bible school training is writing Sunday school materials. "So many are believing, we had to do something," he explained holding out a copy of next month's Bible lessons for us to examine.

"How do you get these lessons printed?" I asked. Our friend smiled.

"I get up in the middle of the night and peddle my bike to the house of a printer friend. He is not even a believer, but he is willing to take the risk. He prints the materials in the wee hours of the morning when most of the police are off the streets."

Jim and I were keenly aware that our friend

had already been in prison for over six years for his boldness in preaching the gospel. His only comment about himself was: "We are unafraid, but we are prayerful!"

And in a stark prison cell only a few miles from our hotel was the "pastor with the little boy face." This is the name which the communist chose to give Pastor Ho Hieu Ha. Ministering at the former International Church, Pastor Ha led 5,000 to Christ, 2,000 of whom were baptized right on the church property. Of necessity there were twenty-one services a week. This anointed servant of God had become so influential in the city that the communists just did not know what to do with him. So they arrested him.

Several years later in exile in California, our pastor friend reflected on his experiences in his wretched prison cell. Pastor Ha told us that his desire to preach and share Christ with his fellow prisoners almost consumed him. The fact that he was locked in solitary confinement did not squelch his zeal at all. In fact, God enabled him to witness to prisoners, teach them Bible verses and even teach them to sing!

"How was this possible, Pastor Ha? In your isolation cell you could not possibly see the prisoner in the next cell much less communicate with prisoners below or above you," we asked.

"I know, but God provided me with a special PA system—the 'squat pot' pipes. It was an already-installed plumbing system which made a natural duct for amplifying sound. And it worked. I prayed with fellow prisoners to receive Christ right through the toilet pipes!" In this manner, Pastor Ha had led ninety-seven inmates to accept Christ.

"Oh, it was so sweet!" he said.

These are the ones—"those" people of Psalm 126—"those who go forth weeping bearing precious seed": the pioneers, those that followed the pioneers—all our colleagues of the "second wave," the martyrs, the gallant Vietnamese pastors. Also in that awesome number is an evangelist who led one small child to the Lord many years ago in Birmingham, Alabama and a high school student who invited her pal to a prayer meeting.

In this group of honorable ones, there are simple fishermen who brought the sick and hurting to the foot of the cross, a doctor who did eye surgery on ailing peasants, a nightclub singer now born again and singing a new song to the glory of God. These are all part of this awesome and inspiring company of God's distinguished servants who "went forth bearing precious seeds." And in every case and hundreds of others like them, there is a returning with joy and arms laden with precious sheaves.

Jim and I are proud to stand with that number. Sure, there have been tears and there have been fears, times when the power of the evil one for some unknown reason seemed to be allowed to attack. But we still go forth because we know that the paths of the Lord, though sometimes strewn with sharp stones and sandspurs, are always laden with His loving-kindness.

And one more thing we found to be true, be it in the madness of war, in a hospital or a classroom—wherever God leads His own, there is a place of peace. No calling in the world is more joyful than that of the sower who goes out with the precious seed of the gospel and later returns with his sheaves of redeemed souls. To God be the glory!

Looking back over the years, Jim and I are thankful to say there has always been far more joy than pain, far more laughter than tears—and, with it all, the sheaves.

> *"Those who sow in tears will reap*
> *with songs of joy.*
> *He who goes out weeping,*
> *carrying seed to sow,*
> *will return with songs of joy,*
> *carrying sheaves with him."*
> (Psalm 126:5-6)

Epilogue

Closure! A new-ish kind of a word, but new faces, new recipes, new books and even new usages of old words seem to be the way things are at furlough time.

"Jean and Jim, here you are at the end of a long missionary career. How do you feel about closure?"

The question was asked in all seriousness, but we were having trouble with its interpretation.

Closure! I think of the signing of a real estate deal. I think of the last phase of delicate surgery. But to my amazement, my friends were not talking about that sort of thing at all, but about the conclusion of our mission work!

Thus it became necessary for me to pause and evaluate this phase of life into which Jim and I have just set foot. We must step back and ask, "Are there no more Vietnamese people to evangelize? Has the last Vietnamese man, woman and child been reached with Tin Lanh? What about the Vietnamese living in St. Petersburg, Tampa, Jacksonville, Orlando, Atlanta or in hundreds of cities all across the United States and Canada?

Yes, our opportunities for missionary work overseas may have closed, but wherever there are Vietnamese people, there is sowing and reaping to be done.

We have touched the lives of thousands of refugees in the past decade. We find them in churches all across the land. But we are not blind to the fact that perhaps hundreds of new converts have been pressed into the American lifestyle and shortly after their arrival in the Beautiful Land have slipped through the net.

We have a vision. It is not a new idea, but simply a continuation of that as yet unfinished task called the Great Commission. We still want to reach Vietnamese for Christ.

With a prayer for that special Holy Spirit anointing, we step forth into a ministry of evangelism and renewal to Vietnamese churches across the east and southwest. We feel that our Tin Lanh churches need to be reached again and again, for there is a need to resist again and again the curse of nominal Christianity and materialism which is creeping into our churches. Our strong desire is to bring to these churches the message of sanctification and spiritual victory that comes through a Spirit-filled life.

Lord, lead us to hungry hearts, to those who came to know
you at the refugee camps in Southeast Asia. Lord, use us to
begin renewal to Vietnamese churches. Lord, make us living
stones, helping to build the Church of the
Living God among the Vietnamese people
even here in the United States. We just do
not have time for closure.

Jim and Jean Livingston reside in Inverness, Florida. They have four grown children.

Steven married Becky Lay, an MK from Indonesia. They have three children—Allison, Christopher and Lindsay. They served as teachers and principal at Dalat School for thirteen years and at present are living in Katy, Texas.

Kim Hoa married David Collins, an MK from Vietnam. They have three children—Melody, Nathan and Angela. They served four years as missionaries in Thailand and the Philippines. Currently, David is director of Food for the Hungry of Canada.

Mona is an emergency room nurse. She married Rev. Carl Morton of the Free Methodist Church, now serving a church near Detroit, Michigan. They have three children—Justin, Kendra and Krissa.

Tara married Tom Chapman and they have two daughters—Haleigh and Jordan. Tom is a product manager with Air Liquide. They are actively involved in the Parkway Fellowship Alliance Church of Houston, Texas.